KU-527-148

To Alice and Thomas; Freya and Adam

Contents

List of tables and figures

Tables

Figures

General abbreviations

AGO	Attorney General's Office
BAME	Black and minority ethnic
CCRC	Criminal Cases Review Commission
CJJI	Criminal Justice Joint Inspectorate
CPS	Crown Prosecution Service
CRC	Community rehabilitation company
DPP	Director of Public Prosecutions
HMCTS	Her Majesty's Courts and Tribunals Service
HMIC	Her Majesty's Inspectorate of Constabulary, (HMICFRS since July 2017)
HMICFRS	Her Majesty's Inspectorate of Constabulary and Fire & Rescue Services
HMI Prisons	Her Majesty's Inspectorate of Prisons for England and Wales
HMI Probation	Her Majesty's Inspectorate of Probation
HMPPS	Her Majesty's Prison and Probation Service
IPCC	Independent Police Complaints Commission
JAC	Judicial Appointments Commission
MAPPA	Multi-agency public protection arrangements
MOJ	Ministry of Justice
MPS	Metropolitan Police Service
NOMS	National Offender Management Service
NPS	National Probation Service
PACE	Police and Criminal Evidence Act 1984
PCSO	Police community support officer

PQiP	Professional Qualification in Probation
SCS	Statutory Charging Scheme

About the authors

Dr Lisa O'Malley is a Senior Lecturer in Social Policy in the Department of Social Policy and Social Work at the University of York, where she teaches Introducing Criminal Justice, Policing and Youth Justice to undergraduate students. Her research interests are primarily concerned with the intersection between crime and social policy, including the relationship between housing tenure and crime, the criminalisation of place and community safety.

Sharon Elizabeth Grace is a Lecturer in the Department of Social Policy and Social Work at the University of York. She teaches specialist modules on illicit drug use and victimisation as well as leading the core criminology and criminal justice modules. Her research interests lie within both criminal justice and drug policy and practice particularly as they relate to women with complex needs.

Preface

The origins of this book lie in our development of crime and criminal justice teaching in the University of York's Social Policy Department. In 2005, just the two of us started with a completely blank page. Some 13 years later, we teach on two exciting and lively programmes of study (BA Social Policy, Crime and Criminal Justice; and BA Criminology). This book therefore represents those 13 years of work in developing core criminal justice teaching and learning; and in thinking about how to make learning about criminal justice interesting and engaging, while ensuring that students clearly understand how the criminal justice system works (or doesn't). Without the engagement of all those students over the years, learning from them and with them, this book would not have been possible, and we thank them for their lively discussions, probing questions and innovative ideas. The faults in the book lie with us.

Lisa O'Malley
Sharon Grace
York, 2017

ONE

Introduction

Criminal. Justice. System. Three words – each of which might merit a whole book in its own right and each of which might conjure up very different definitions, values and expectations. Together they describe one of the largest enterprises of the state, costing around £34 billion per year, employing around 300,000 people, investigating around 4 million reported crimes each year, prosecuting 1.5 million suspects and holding around 85,000 individuals in custody at any one time. But how does this system operate, how are resources distributed across its functions and what kinds of issues face the people who work in this system and those it serves? These questions are addressed in subsequent chapters of this short guide. In this introductory chapter, the aim is to say a little more about some of the key terms and themes that provide the context to later discussions.

What do we mean by criminal justice? The answer to this question will vary depending on someone's interest in the subject and, possibly, the kind of work they are undertaking. For most students, the study of criminal justice sits alongside wider programmes of knowledge that might comprise criminology, sociology, social policy, politics, and so on. As such, the study of criminal justice might involve understanding the purpose and function of different agencies as well as engaging with debates about how the system works or could work better. For those who work within the agencies of the criminal justice system, definitions of 'justice' may be less important than the need to meet targets or work within rules and guidelines that are decided by national governments, or sometimes international bodies and over which individual employees may have little control. As a suspect, the term criminal justice may take on special significance – especially if you are not guilty of a crime or believe there are factors that should be taken into account about why you committed an offence. In these circumstances, your perception of 'justice' is likely to be heavily influenced by how you are treated by people working in the agencies of the system, and whether you accept or agree with the outcome of your case. Similar issues might influence victims' views of criminal justice, where finding out 'who' committed the crime and seeing justice done (most often in the form of punishment) might be most important.

Clearly then, criminal justice means different things to different people – its meaning will vary through time and space, and the way criminal justice is delivered and organised will similarly vary according to cultural and political priorities. As such, criminal justice can be highly contested and interpreted and understood very differently depending on political, ideological or philosophical views. Yet at the same time the idea of a criminal justice system suggests a set of administrative functions that are concerned with the processing of 'criminals', and it is with these functions and processes that the remainder of this book is primarily concerned.

Themes that help us to understand criminal justice

Criminal justice and the rule of law

In most western nations, the idea of justice is linked to values of fairness, democracy, human rights and the rule of law. The latter is a useful starting point for thinking about the kinds of principles that might underpin the operation of a 'justice system'. Rule of law signifies the supremacy of the law of the land over any other authority, and is applicable to all citizens regardless of their status. Most importantly, perhaps, the rule of law means that punishment and rights should only be meted out in accordance with clearly defined rules and procedures (see Box 1.1: Bingham's eight principles of the rule of law). How far the UK criminal justice system upholds these principles remains open to question, but they do point to some of the aspirations we might have for our criminal justice system and some of the ways we might begin to critically assess its effectiveness.

Box 1.1: Eight principles of the rule of law

1. The law must be accessible and so far as possible, intelligible, clear and predictable
2. Questions of legal right and liability should ordinarily be resolved by application of the law and not the exercise of discretion
3. The laws of the land should apply equally to all, save to the extent that objective differences justify differentiation
4. Ministers and public officers at all levels must exercise the powers conferred on them in good faith, fairly, for the purpose for which the powers were conferred, without exceeding the limits of such powers and not unreasonably
5. The law must afford adequate protection of fundamental human rights
6. Means must be provided for resolving without prohibitive cost or inordinate delay, bona fide civil disputes which the parties themselves are unable to resolve
7. Adjudicative procedures provided by the state should be fair
8. The rule of law requires compliance by the state with its obligations in international law as in national law

Source: Bingham, 2010

Models of criminal justice

Sets of principles like those produced by Lord Bingham might be aspirational, but they do little to help us to understand how the priorities or activities of criminal justice might be organised or delivered. One of the most enduring models of criminal justice systems derives from Herbert Packer's (1968) *The limits of the criminal sanction*, which describes two ideal types of criminal justice: **'due process'** and **'crime control'** (see Box 1.2). An example of due process-oriented policy making might include the rules surrounding stop and search, arrest and detention by the police (commonly referred to as PACE – see Chapter Two), which intends to provide a transparent set of procedures for police officers to follow, while crime control-oriented policy might include the right to hold terrorist suspects without charge. In the former example, suspects have rights that are intended to protect them from unlawful prosecution or punishment, whereas in the latter example fear of crime and public demands might lead to innocent people losing their freedom. The issue here is perhaps one of degree or the extent to which either of these models takes priority in policy and practice. The evidence presented in this book tends towards an exploration of the administrative functions and overall policy aims of the criminal justice system (*how* things are done), which might be at odds with expectations of the system (how things *should* be done); or the reasons for certain styles of operation (*why* things are done). Hence, models of justice are useful, because they allow us to interrogate the purpose of policy and practice in criminal justice and go some way to explaining why our justice system sometimes seems to reflect competing aims and objectives.

Box 1.2: Features of due process and crime control models of criminal justice

Due process:

- emphasises the application of rules and procedures that are publicly known, fair and transparent;
- main function of the court is to act as an impartial arbitrator;
- prioritises civil liberties in order to ensure that the innocent are acquitted.

Crime control:

- emphasises that the primary function of criminal justice is to control crime by punishing offenders;
- courts are seen as guardians of law and order and emphasis is on efficient processes for conviction;
- prioritises conviction of the guilty, even at the risk of civil liberties being infringed.

Politics and criminal justice

Since the 1970s, successive governments have sought to show the public that they are tough on crime, and it would be almost inconceivable in 2017 to imagine a general election where no one talked about crime or the police service or prisons or young offenders in some form or another. As such, we can describe the criminal justice system as 'politicised'. There is not space in this text to explore the politics of each agency in detail, but a brief summary of some of the main trends in approaches to criminal justice that can be discerned in the period since 1945 should help you to place some of the subsequent debates within a wider sociopolitical context:

- **1945–70** – bi-partisan consensus characterised by a 'penal-welfare' approach that prioritised ideals of rehabilitation and treatment to reform offenders. Crime was a marginal political issue; where concern was raised, this was mostly in relation to juvenile offending.

- ■ **1970s** – Breakdown of consensus across political parties as the Conservative party blamed Labour governments for economic crisis and rising industrial disorder that provided the backdrop for rising crime rates. Influential ideas that 'nothing works' in relation to rehabilitation, combined with a more general loss of faith in the general principles of welfarist approaches to social policy, paved the way for increasing political interest in criminal justice management and organisation.

- ■ **1980–92** – Conservative administrations through the 1980s introduced a raft of reforms of the public sector that also affected criminal justice agencies. Among the most notable was the introduction of managerialist principles, including performance management through the setting of targets and the drive for 'efficiency' and value for money (see Box 1.3). However, these changes did not affect government spending on criminal justice, which continued to rise – particularly in the police service, where Conservative administrations believed stronger policing remained the answer to law and order problems.

- ■ **1993–2010** – a new consensus emerged across major political parties around the priorities for the criminal justice system. It included: the targeting of dangerous and persistent offenders; a belief in 'multi-agency' working to reduce crime; a focus on incivility (exemplified by approaches to anti-social behaviour); and the continuing influence of managerialist principles that created an increasingly 'mixed economy' of service delivery (to be discussed later). A key feature of criminal justice politics in this period was the rise of 'penal populism' – a belief by political parties that success in general elections depends on showing a tough approach to law and order.

- ■ **2010 to the present** – the electioneering around criminal justice policy began to wane after the financial crisis of 2008, and the three elections since 2010 have seen much less focus on law and order than previously. In the face of increasingly tough fiscal measures designed to reduce the public finance deficit, criminal justice agencies have been treated in the same way as other public services and subject to draconian budget cuts of up to 25% in some instances. This has meant that the drive for efficiency and cost saving has begun to dominate discussions about how the criminal justice system might be reformed, as subsequent chapters demonstrate.

Box 1.3: New public management principles in criminal justice

- Increased emphasis on achieving results rather than administering processes
- The setting of explicit targets and performance indicators to enable auditing of efficiency and effectiveness
- The publication of league tables illustrating comparative performance
- The identification of core competencies
- The costing and market testing of all activities to ensure value for money
- The externalisation of non-essential responsibilities
- The establishment of a purchaser-provider split
- The encouragement of inter-agency co-operation
- The re-designation of clients as 'customers'

Source: McLaughlin et al, 2001, p 302

A mixed economy of criminal justice

One of the consequences of new public management principles in criminal justice has been a 'rolling back of the state' in direct service provision. This chapter started by suggesting that concepts of justice and the rule of law were central to understanding how criminal justice systems could or should be organised. These principles say very little about 'who' should deliver these services, and it is quite easy to assume that public order and security remains a state or publicly provided function. This is simply no longer the case. The criminal justice system, like many areas of welfare provision, reflects a 'mixed economy' of service delivery that now incorporates public, private and non-profit elements across all its functions. The chapters that follow highlight the main aspects of criminal justice delivery that are affected by these shifts and the implications arising from them, most specifically in Chapter Five (prison privatisation) and Chapter Seven (privatisation of probation services).

This mixed economy of provision also encompasses increasing emphasis on multi-agency and partnership working in the management of crime. Much of this happens at a local level, where community safety partnerships (formerly crime and disorder reduction partnerships) are required to develop plans for tackling crime. The police and probation services are designated responsible authorities in these partnerships, reflecting the role that they are expected to play in managing offenders in the community. They work alongside colleagues from health services, the local authority and fire and rescue services to develop local crime plans and approaches to dealing with criminal behaviour.

The challenges faced by criminal justice agencies in working in multi-agency partnerships are discussed in more detail in the concluding chapter, but as you work through the following chapters, it is worth considering the extent to which assumptions about the benefits of multi-agency working are embedded within criminal justice practices.

The relationship between crime and criminal justice

The focus of this book is on those aspects of crime and offending behaviour that come to the attention of the relevant authorities. It is, therefore, a book about how people whose actions have been defined as criminal are treated by the agencies that have been empowered to deal with them on behalf of the state. It would be wrong to interpret this as anything like a system that is designed to deal with 'crime' – rather, it is a system designed to deal with 'law breakers'. The distinction is important for a number of reasons.

First, it is important to remember that only a very small proportion of all crime is dealt with through formal criminal justice processes. There are, therefore, a large number of criminal acts (and hence offenders) that are never reported, investigated, or counted in official statistics.

Second, the criminal justice system relies upon a specific – and some would argue very narrow – definition of what constitutes a crime, relying on legal definitions of around 1,500 types of 'notifiable offences' (those that the police have a statutory duty to record), potentially ignoring or omitting acts that generate serious harm but are not defined as 'crime'.

Third, critics of this kind of legalistic definition of crime would also argue that it limits the scope of the criminal justice system to deal with all types of offenders – particularly those who commit 'white collar' crime and corporate crime. It is useful to maintain a critical gaze on how far the operations of the criminal justice system might be able to address these issues – or whether, indeed, it would be feasible or necessary to do so.

Discretion, discrimination and inequality in criminal justice

The criminal justice system does not treat all those who come into contact with it in the same way. The police do not always arrest offenders, the Crown Prosecution Service does not always proceed with cases, and judges do not always pass the same sentence for similar offences. Understanding why these differences occur, and using evidence of differences in practices to engage critically with aspects of unequal outcomes in the criminal justice system, requires us to consider four interrelated concepts that are frequently referred to by commentators and researchers: namely discretion, discrimination, disproportionality and inequality.

Discretion

The term 'discretion' refers to the freedom, power or authority that an individual has to use their own judgement when deciding upon what action to take in a given situation (for example, whether to arrest someone or send them to prison). In most areas of criminal justice, rules or guidelines exist that are intended to provide agencies and their staff with clarity about these actions (for example having evidence to arrest someone, or using sentencing guidelines to decide on appropriate sentences), but these rules and guidelines often provide agencies with flexibility in how they are applied depending on circumstances. This flexibility can prevent rules being applied inappropriately – the phrase 'letter of the law' is often used to imply an inflexible approach to a situation where rules guide actions without any consideration of circumstances – but it is also the case that the application of discretion is closely linked to discrimination and potential injustice: 'It is the day to day discretionary actions of police officers, prosecutors, defence lawyers, judges, psychiatrists, prison, probation and immigration officers, among others, which are the stuff of justice and which make for justice or injustice' (Gelsthorpe and Padfield, 2003, p1).

Discrimination

The lack of clear guidelines or scrutiny of decision making that might increase the scope for discretion, also has implications for discrimination, because the capacity for discretion allows the potential for decisions to be made based on prejudicial grounds. The term 'discrimination' refers to the treatment of individuals based on race, gender, class, religion, sexual orientation, disability and so on, in ways that are unfavourable. Although all agencies of the criminal justice system are bound by legislation that prevents discriminatory practice (for example Race Relations (Amendment) Act 2000, Equality Act 2010), the unwritten, preconceived ideas that might shape an individual's views have major implications for the application of 'justice' when they are combined with high levels of discretion. An example that is often used in criminal justice practices refers to the evidence of discrimination against black males in stop and search practices by the police (see Chapter Three).

Disproportionality

It is very difficult to prove that criminal justice agencies are systematically engaging in discriminatory practices against particular social groups, or that discretion is used to support discrimination by individual officers. In attempting to highlight unequal outcomes for different social groups, the term 'disproportionality' is used to describe the under- or over-representation of a particular social group within the criminal justice compared to the general population.

In the criminal justice system, disproportionality occurs at all stages of the process in relation to race and social class; people from black and minority ethnic populations and lower social classes are over-represented in the criminal justice system. Specific aspects of disproportionality are also reflected in prison populations – for example in relation to lower educational attainment, experience of mental health problems and experience of the care system as a child (see Chapter Six).

Inequality

The term 'inequality' is used in this text to describe more general aspects of differential treatment of offenders (and victims) despite similar circumstances. Sometimes that might be because discrimination is occurring, or it might be simply that the system does not allow different circumstances to be take into account. The idea that we are all 'equal before the law' remains a powerful tenet of our justice system, but the inconsistent application of rules and guidelines can create inequality, unfairness and consequently injustice.

How to use this book

The chapters that follow aim to provide a succinct description of each of the main agencies of the criminal justice system in England and Wales, in the order that an offender (or a case) might be processed. The focus on England and Wales provides consistency across each chapter in a short text, but significant differences in criminal justice in Scotland and Northern Ireland are referred to, where it is most relevant and appropriate.

The content also focuses on adult offenders (those aged over 18 years), and primarily male adult offenders, although we draw attention to aspects of inequality relating to female offenders where this is particularly relevant.

Each chapter adopts a similar structure, so that issues can be compared across agencies as well as providing an introduction to each agency in particular. Each chapter introduces a number of 'key debates and issues' that students may wish to explore further, and that reflect current policy and practice concerns. The choice of these issues is necessarily subjective, but is driven mostly by a concern to reflect some of the broad themes that have been introduced in the sections mentioned earlier. A final section in each chapter aims to draw out aspects of discretion, discrimination and inequality as they are experienced by offenders or those working in the criminal justice system, by using specific examples or topics for further analysis.

One of the aims of this text is to introduce ways of analysing criminal justice policy and practice that overlap with other areas of public policy. The themes we have chosen to focus on therefore parallel debates in other areas of social policy, and we hope to inspire students from all social science disciplines to bring the same analytic focus to criminal justice policy, as they do to other areas of policy and practice.

However, criminal justice is a fast-moving area of public policy and practice. As such, the administration, guidelines and statistics referred to in textbooks is often out of date before it is even published. Consequently, each chapter includes suggestions for further reading and a list of websites where students can access the most up-to-date information and statistics about each of the agencies, so that the tables and figures we have included here can be updated easily, and our interpretation and analysis scrutinised for ongoing relevance.

Chapter Two begins with a broad overview of the criminal justice system, and uses an example of an offender's journey to highlight some of the key decision-making points that occur through the process. This is followed by individual chapters on the police service, the Crown Prosecution Service, the court system, the prison service and probation.

A concluding chapter revisits the themes introduced here to consider the evidence presented throughout the book.

Taking it further ...

More in-depth reading about the issues raised in this chapter

Downes, D. and Morgan, R. (2002) The skeletons in the cupboard: The politics of law and order at the turn of the millennium, in M. Maguire, R. Morgan and R. Reiner (eds) *Oxford handbook of criminology* (3rd edn), Oxford: Oxford University Press

Gelsthorpe, L. and Padfield, N. (2003) *Exercising discretion: Decision making in the criminal justice system and beyond*, Cullompton: Willan Publishing

Packer, H. (1968) *The limits of the criminal sanction*, Stanford, CA: Stanford University Press

Questions to consider from this chapter and your further reading

- To what extent do you think the principles of law make for a 'just' criminal justice system?
- Should we all be equal before the law?
- What are the positive and negative aspects of discretion in criminal justice decision making?

TWO

The criminal justice process

The criminal justice process and government

Broadly speaking, the criminal justice process can be broken down into five main stages as follows:

- offence/arrest
- charge and prosecution
- trial and hearing
- sentencing
- post-sentencing.

Different agencies and government departments are involved at each stage, and they all have their own specific aims and objectives. The focus in this text is with the five main agencies that deal directly with offenders as follows:

- the police service
- the Crown Prosecution Service
- the criminal courts (comprising Crown Court and magistrates' courts)

■ the prison service
■ the probation service.

Figure 2.1 shows the current organisational structure of the criminal justice system in England and Wales.

Figure 2.1: Organisations of the criminal justice system in England and Wales

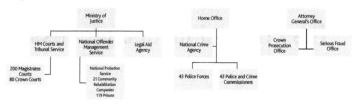

Each agency within the system must work independently from one another in order not to unduly influence each other's decision-making. The government can make new laws, create new criminal offences and allocate funding to the criminal justice system, but it cannot interfere with the independent decisions made by the police, the Crown Prosecution Service (CPS), the magistracy and the judiciary in individual cases. This is not to say that these are the only actors in the criminal process, however. In addition to the activities that are managed through government departments, the criminal justice system relies on a wide range of other actors – notably defence lawyers and a range of private and voluntary sector organisations – that provide many of the services on which the main agencies depend, as well as independent 'inspectorates', who play an important role in overseeing the activities of frontline organisations (see Box 2.1).

Box 2.1: The role of inspectorates

There are four main criminal justice inspectorates: Her Majesty's Crown Prosecution Service Inspectorate; Her Majesty's Inspectorate of Constabulary; Her Majesty's Inspectorate of Prisons; and Her Majesty's Inspectorate of Probation. In addition, there is also a Criminal Justice Joint Inspection process, which brings the four individual inspectorates together to work on issues that involve more than one criminal justice agency.

The purpose of these inspectorates is to assess the quality of the work carried out by these agencies in order to improve efficiency and effectiveness and to promote justice and fairness in criminal proceedings. Inspectorate reports will make recommendations to the agencies aimed at improving the effectiveness of their services and may well conduct follow-up inspections to see if these recommendations have been taken on board. An inspection will involve: the examination of files or other documentation; the distribution of questionnaires or surveys; direct observations; and interviews with service users or other key stakeholders. Inspectorates' findings are published and presented to those in positions of political or executive power, to enable an independent way to hold criminal justice agencies to account and to contribute to policy development.

Government departments and the criminal justice process

The Home Office – from offence to arrest

The role of Home Secretary is considered one of the great offices of state, dating back to 1782. The current Home Secretary (Amber Rudd, since 2016) is only the third female to hold the office – the first was Jacqui Smith in 2007. Since 1945 there have been 27 Home Secretaries, serving 14 different Prime Ministers (a full list can be found in Appendix 1). Until relatively recently, the Home Office was responsible for most of the frontline activities of the criminal justice system, but since 2007 it is only the police service that remains under direct control of the Home Secretary. Other criminal justice functions are now the responsibility of the Ministry of Justice (MOJ) and the Attorney General's Office (AGO). The key responsibilities of the Home Office relate primarily to security and policing issues, but it remains a powerful presence in criminal justice, not least because it controls budgets for individual police forces and sets the agenda for priorities in relation to crime control and crime prevention. In relation to the stages of the criminal justice process, the Home Office has primary responsibility for offence/arrest through control of policing. The Home Office is also responsible for the activities of the National Crime Agency, which is mostly involved with dealing with serious and organised crime.

The Attorney General's Office – charge and prosecution

The AGO provides legal advice and support to the Attorney General and the Solicitor General (the Law Officers). Through its management of the CPS, the AGO is central to the charge and prosecution stage of the criminal justice process as well as the trial itself, where prosecutions are brought on behalf of the state. The AGO can also be asked to review individual sentence decisions that are deemed very low or unduly lenient, and it can take legal action in the public interest if certain types of contempt of court have been committed. In reality, however, the AGO itself is rarely involved in individual cases – instead, responsibility for charge and prosecution is devolved to the CPS.

The Ministry of Justice – from trial to post-sentencing

The MOJ's responsibilities in relation to stages of criminal justice process start at the point of trial – once a case has come to court – through to post-sentencing stages that might involve the prison or probation services. When it was created in 2007, the MOJ absorbed the responsibilities of the (then) Department for Constitutional Affairs (previously the Lord Chancellor's Department) and took on many previous Home Office responsibilities for courts, prisons, parole and probation. In addition, the MOJ has executive responsibility for the Youth Justice Board, the Legal Aid Agency and the Office of the Public Guardian. The Ministry is overseen by the Justice Secretary appointed by the Prime Minister. To date, there have only been seven Ministers of Justice (see Appendix 2 for a full list) and the post is yet to achieve a status to match that of Home Secretary, despite being responsible for key aspects of justice including sentencing and punishment.

The aims of the MOJ are most often framed in relatively wide terms (for example to protect the public and to reduce reoffending), which can be achieved in any number of ways – from punitive approaches that seek to protect the public by increasing the use of custodial sentences, to rehabilitation models that seek to reform offenders (see Chapter Six).

As such, the activities of the MOJ, as with all government departments, are subject to political and economic decision-making beyond its control, so while the legal and administrative functions of agencies involved in the criminal justice system are important on their own, it is important to be mindful of the political context within which these operate.

2000 Criminal Justice and Court Services Act

The criminal justice system in numbers

The cost of criminal justice

Each criminal justice agency system produces its own annual report that provides details of its activities and expenditure for the year. These figures can be used to interrogate the costs of criminal justice: the reported expenditure for 2015/16 is captured in Figure 2.2.

Figure 2.2: Proportion of total expenditure by agency

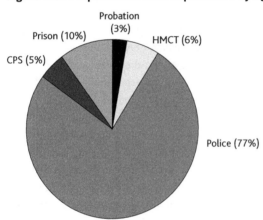

Despite playing a crucial role in decisions about charging and prosecution, the CPS accounts for just 5% of expenditure. The costs of providing policing (which provides a crime prevention as well as a detection function) represent 77% of expenditure across the agencies included in this book, with the wide-ranging functions of the MOJ representing 44% of total expenditure. These costs can be put into some context by comparing them to other areas of welfare spending, using data from the Government Budget Estimates for 2016–17: the costs of providing public order and safety (£34 billion) are dwarfed by those for health (£145 billion), education (£102 billion) and social protection (£240 billion), but are more than that spent on personal social services (£30 billion) and transport (£29 billion).

Expenditure on criminal justice is highly dependent on a range of factors beyond the control of individual government departments, most notably in relation to crime rates themselves but also as a result of wider government policy. So, for example, it would be unsurprising to find criminal justice costs rising, if a government pursues particularly punitive policies with regard to crime (as more people are arrested and sentenced to imprisonment perhaps). This is not to suggest that non-punitive approaches are 'cheaper', however – high-quality rehabilitation and resettlement programmes can be more expensive than regimes that seek only to punish. However, the cost-effectiveness of rehabilitation is often used to justify the higher cost – if it is possible to prevent someone from reoffending, then potentially the state will save money in the long run. So, when we are thinking about costs of criminal justice, and the impact of government policies, it is always worth thinking about the financial implications – very costly interventions, no matter how well evidenced, are unlikely to be popular with politicians who are trying to balance the books.

Working in the criminal justice system

Adopting a broad view of the agencies and organisations involved in delivering and administering the criminal justice system, it is estimated that around 300,000 people are employed across the public and private sector. More specifically, the public sector agencies covered in the following chapters employ around 176,000 people in frontline delivery activities. Figure 2.3 shows the proportions of employees in each main agency, and reflects a similar distribution of human resource as the expenditure data in Figure 2.2, with the police ranks representing the largest proportion at 57% (124,000 police officers); and the CPS the smallest at 3% (6,000 people).

Figure 2.3: Proportions of workforce by agency, 2016

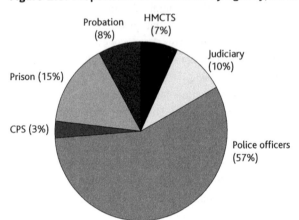

These overall figures belie considerable differences in the demographic profile of agency staff – an issue that is of concern to those who argue that the criminal justice system should be 'representative' of the community it serves. Key arguments in this regard are raised in relation to the police service, where low proportions of officers from black and minority ethnic groups has frequently been seen as a barrier to generating better relationships between the police and ethnic minority communities (see Chapter Three). Similar arguments are sometimes levied at the judiciary in relation to the high proportions of white, male judges from privileged backgrounds (see Chapter Five). Each of the following chapters provides a profile of staffing in relation to gender and ethnicity as a guide to the key differences across agencies, and in the concluding chapter further discussion about aspects of inequality and disproportionality in the workforce are explored (see Chapter Eight).

Aside from those formally employed in the agencies themselves, a vast number of individuals are employed by private and voluntary organisations that are also engaged in delivering criminal justice in a mixed economy (see Chapter One). The public and voluntary sector organisations are further supported by a small army of volunteers, who offer unpaid support in a variety of roles, many of which are open to anyone to get involved (see Box 2.2).

Box 2.2: Volunteering in the criminal justice system

There are vast numbers of people engaged in voluntary work within the criminal justice system. The following list is not exhaustive, but gives an indication of the range of activities that people undertake in different areas:

- **supporting victims of crime** – victim support in the community and through the Victim Supportline; witness support in court
- **supporting offenders in the community** – mentoring; MAPPA lay adviser;
- **supporting prisoners** – Samaritans listeners; prison visitors; independent monitoring board members;
- **supporting prisoners' children and families** – court workers; family befrienders; family and visitor centres within prison;
- **police, prosecution and crime prevention** – police support volunteers; independent custody visitors; local scrutiny and involvement panel member; appropriate adults;
- **faith-based volunteer work** – chaplaincy services (and equivalents); street patrols.

Source: Prison Reform Trust, 2017

2013 Transforming Rehabilitation White Paper 2014 Offender Rehabilitation Act

Offenders and disproportionality in the criminal justice system

The scale of the justice system can also be represented by the overall caseload. The MOJ produces quarterly statistics that summarises the 'flow' of cases through the system. Data for 2016 shows that 1.7 million individuals were dealt with by the criminal justice system, leading to a total of 1.46 million prosecutions, the majority of which are dealt with at the magistrates' court (81%). A total of 89,317 custodial sentences were handed down, and a further 161,454 community sentences were passed. These kinds of statistics are useful for showing the proportions of people who pass through each stage of the criminal justice process and generally reveal a funnelling effect throughout the system. The largest number of individual cases are dealt with by the police and the CPS, and the fewest by the prison service, once sentence is passed. Giving a sense of the overall system in this way is particularly useful for examining aspects of differential experience through the justice process – the most controversial of which relates to the experience of black, Asian and minority ethnic (BAME) individuals. Frequently, the proportion of BAME individuals within the criminal justice system is a reflection of the first point of contact – so if the police are disproportionate in the arrest of BAME individuals, then that disproportionality flows through the rest of the process. Table 2.1 should be interpreted with this in mind, but shows the proportion of BAME individuals at different stages of the criminal process, and serves as a reminder that not all people experience the criminal justice system in the same way. The data shows that arrest rates are highest for black individuals at 56 per 1,000 of the population compared with 19 for white individuals. This disproportionality flows through the system through to prisoners, where there are more black and mixed ethnicity individuals in prison compared to other ethnicities per 10,000 of the population.

The persistence of these kinds of data and the concerns they raise about BAME individuals' experience of the criminal justice system led the

Table 2.1: Selected statistics on race and criminal justice, 2014

	Arrest rate (per 1,000 population)	Prosecution (per 1,000 population)	Sentencing (per 1,000 population)	Custody rate	Prisoners (per 10,000 population)	Average custodial sentence length
White	19	6	5	27%	14	17 months
Black	56	18	13	31%	55	25 months
Asian	20	5	4		16	25 months
Mixed	38	11	9		44	20 months
Chinese or other	18	4	4		6	19 months

Source: Ministry of Justice (2015).

then Prime Minister to announce the Lammy Review in January 2016, to investigate the treatment of BAME individuals within the criminal justice system in England and Wales. Data collected and analysed by the MOJ as part of the review identified aspects of disproportionality throughout the criminal justice system – in other words, points in the process where BAME individuals are treated differently to white individuals. The review uses a 'relative rate index' to compare rates of contact with the criminal justice system experienced by different groups, based on an 'at risk' population rather than the general population. This method has the advantage of separating out each stage of the process, because only those 'at risk' of conviction are included in the calculation of conviction disproportionality, for example.

Disproportionality was found to occur at four specific points in the criminal justice process as follows:

1. **Arrest**
- Black men were greater than three times more likely to be arrested than white men.

■ Both black and mixed ethnic women were more than twice as likely to be arrested than white women.

2. Being tried at Crown Court rather than magistrates' court

■ Black (40% more likely) and Asian (62% more likely) men were more likely to be committed to the Crown Court for trial than white men.

■ Black (63% more likely) and mixed ethnic (36% more likely) women were more likely to be committed to the Crown Court for trial than white women, and Asian women more than twice as likely.

3. Custodial remand and plea at Crown Court

■ Black, mixed ethnic and other ethnic men were more than 20% more likely than white men to be remanded in custody.

■ Black, Asian and other minority ethnic men were greater than 50% more likely than white men to plead 'not guilty' at Crown Court.

4. Custodial sentencing

■ Black men were 12% more likely to receive a custodial sentence than white men at Crown Court.

■ Black women were 25% more likely than white women to be sentenced to custody at Crown Court.

These points in the system are particularly significant: arrest marks the entry point to the criminal justice system and further investigation by the police and CPS. Where a trial takes place is also important, because 'mode of trial' decisions can have implications for who decides whether a defendant is guilty and the range of sentencing decisions available to the court (see Box 2.3), including the likelihood of receiving a custodial sentence. Similarly, the conditions for prisoners held on remand is frequently poor (see Chapter Six).

Box 2.3: Mode of trial decisions

In summary or indictable-only offences, the decision as to where the case is held is straightforward. However, where a defendant has been charged with a 'triable either way' offence, the magistrates' court will hold a 'plea before venue and allocation' hearing. At this hearing, the magistrates will decide whether the case will be heard in the magistrates' court or the Crown Court. It is likely that in more complex and/or serious cases, the magistrates will decline jurisdiction and send the case to the Crown Court. Even if they do decide to hear the case but believe that their sentencing powers are too limited, they can send the defendant to the Crown Court for sentencing. In addition, the defendant has the right to elect for jury trial at the Crown Court. The most likely reason a defendant would elect is that they believe they have a better chance of acquittal before a jury.

As you work through subsequent chapters, it is important to remember that disproportionality is experienced by some social groups throughout the criminal justice system, raising important questions about the application of discretion and the impact of unequal treatment – issues that we return to in the concluding chapter.

Stages of the criminal justice process

In England and Wales, the criminal justice process starts with the investigation of an alleged offence, follows through to arrest and prosecution and then to trial and conviction before finally to sentence and sanction – though of course not all cases will result in a conviction. Throughout the process it is important that each stage is carried out using fair and correct procedures and that criminal justice professionals do not abuse or misuse their powers – this principle is known as 'due process' (see Chapter One). It is important to note that the system in Scotland and Northern Ireland operates differently – a summary of the major differences in these jurisdictions is shown in Box 2.4.

Box 2.4: Differences in the criminal justice systems of Scotland and Northern Ireland

Scotland has had an independent criminal justice system since the 1707 Act of Union. Following devolution and the 1998 Scottish Act, the Scottish Government, through the offices of the Cabinet Secretary for Justice, has overall responsibility for criminal justice policy and procedure. There are 13 publicly managed and two privately managed prisons in Scotland. Since 2013, Scotland has had a single police service – Police Scotland – following the merger of eight regional forces.

Key differences in the Scottish system (compared with that of England and Wales) are:

- Two types of procedure – summary (less serious) and solemn (more serious).
- Three courts:
  - High Court: presided over by a judge to deal with the most serious (solemn) cases;
  - Sheriff Court: presided over by a legally trained Sheriff to deal with cases of intermediate seriousness – both summary and solemn; and
  - Justice of the Peace Court: presided over by lay magistrates to deal with the least serious (summary) cases.
- Prosecutions conducted by the Crown Office and Procurator Fiscal – who have an investigative function and can direct and instruct police investigations.

- Juries of 15 with a simple majority verdict allowed (8/15).
- Three verdicts – guilty, not guilty and not proven.
- No probation service – all 'probation' functions are carried out by criminal justice social workers.

Northern Ireland's criminal justice system is more similar to the system in England and Wales, in that it too has magistrates' courts and a Crown Court. It has one police service – the Police Service for Northern Ireland, which replaced the Royal Ulster Constabulary in 2001 as part of the Good Friday Agreement. It has its own prosecution service, the Public Prosecutions Service for Northern Ireland, established in 2002. Prosecutors work with the police in the same way as in England and Wales, and do not have an investigative role. All probation officers working for the Probation Board for Northern Ireland are qualified social workers.

Box 2.5 outlines the fictitious case of 'Jimmy', whose journey through the criminal justice process is then described in more detail. However, Jimmy's journey is necessarily selective – the aim here is to highlight some of the key areas of decision making that occur within the process, when and by whom. A full legalistic account of all the options available to decision makers in this case is beyond the scope of this book, but Jimmy's example does serve to identify the key rights to which suspects are entitled.

Box 2.5: Case study example – Jimmy Clayton

Jimmy was born in Liverpool and has lived all his life on the Highbrook estate – a council estate in the Old Swan area. He is white British, and at the time of his arrest was aged 32 and had been married to Lorraine for 14 years. He has two children, Jordan, aged 14 and Carmel, aged 10. He left school at 16 with two GCSEs and has since worked on building sites as a labourer. Work has always been intermittent, depending on how the building trade is going. Jimmy is very sociable and has always enjoyed a drink with his mates on a Friday night, if the wage packet allows it. He drinks fairly heavily, but no more than any of his mates, but he can be aggressive when he has had a few pints.

On 15 December 2008, Jimmy got into a fight with Steve Jones outside a nightclub in town. Jimmy allegedly stamped on Steve's head several times, which resulted in Steve sustaining a fractured skull. Steve spent four weeks in hospital – two of them in intensive care. This was Jimmy's first arrest for a serious violent crime. He has three previous convictions: a public order offence from his late teens; and a criminal damage and common assault from his early twenties – since which time he has not been in trouble with police.

Jimmy pleaded not guilty to Section 18 (of the Offences Against the Person Act 1861) Grievous Bodily Harm with intent. He was found guilty following a trial at the Crown Court and was sentenced to 10 years' imprisonment. He served six years in custody before being released on licence in 2015 to serve the remaining four years of his sentence under the supervision of the National Probation Service. During his time in prison, his marriage ended and he left prison with no secure accommodation and no employment.

All criminal cases start with the **police** action. The police decide who should enter the system as a suspect and then must investigate the case, interview the suspect, gather corroborative evidence and, often in partnership with the CPS (see Chapter Four), charge the suspect where they have sufficient evidence to do so. The police can also decide to: take no further action in a case; 'no-crime' a case (where they believe a crime has not taken place); or caution or fine an offender, in which instance the case is then finalised and does not move forward to court proceedings. As a result of the Police and Criminal Evidence Act 1984 (PACE) and its associated Codes of Practice (see Chapter Three), there are a series of safeguards that should protect the rights of a suspect during their time in police custody.

In our case study, Jimmy was arrested and cautioned outside the nightclub and taken to a designated police station with a custody sergeant, who oversaw his detention. The custody sergeant holds the key responsibility for ensuring that Jimmy's rights under PACE are adhered to during his time in custody, including: whether there is sufficient evidence to charge Jimmy; whether his continuing detention is justified; whether he is being treated properly in terms of length of interviews and suitable breaks; medical attention; provision of food and water; and whether he is at any risk of suicide or self-harm. While he is at the station, the police are permitted to interview Jimmy and retrieve samples of DNA from him, and to take his fingerprints and his photograph – in order to establish his identification. Jimmy can be held for up to 96 hours before being charged, though beyond 24 hours, approval will have to be sought to do so from an officer of superintendent level or above.

The custody sergeant will also inform Jimmy of his rights under PACE, which are:

- *the right to legal advice;*
- *the right to tell someone he has been arrested;*

- ■ *the right to medical help;*
- ■ *the right to an appropriate adult (if under 17 or mentally impaired);*
- ■ *the right to consult the Codes of Practice;*
- ■ *the right to be told of his rights (such as regular breaks and refreshments);*
- ■ *the right to decent conditions;*
- ■ *the right to silence.*

In England and Wales, everyone arrested and taken to a police station for questioning is entitled to legal representation, free of charge, 24 hours a day. The Duty Solicitor Scheme provides these legal advisers if the suspect does not have their own solicitor. Similarly, there are also duty solicitors at magistrates' courts, if the defendant does not have legal representation. In very minor cases, defendants may choose to represent themselves. Defence solicitors and barristers are not state agents, but their role in the criminal justice system is crucial in ensuring that suspects' and defendants' rights are protected and their interests are represented at the police station and at court.

*Once Jimmy has been interviewed under caution and the police have gathered other corroborative evidence, they will move to charge. The decision on the most appropriate charge in Jimmy's case will be done in conjunction with a prosecutor from the **CPS**. In this case, the evidence against Jimmy included CCTV footage from outside the nightclub and eyewitness accounts, and Jimmy was charged with Section 18 Grievous Bodily Harm with intent. Once the police have charged Jimmy, they will decide whether to bail him to appear at court at a later date or to bring him immediately before the magistrates.*

The CPS conducts the prosecution of the defendant and continually reviews a case up to the point where it reaches court. Using the Code for Crown Prosecutors (see Chapter Four), the prosecutor will review all the evidence available and decide whether there is sufficient evidence to take a case to court, and whether it is in the public interest to do so.

Jimmy has been charged with an indictable-only offence, which means that his trial must be heard at the Crown Court (see Box 2.6). However, as with all other criminal offences, Jimmy must first appear at the magistrates' courts. At the first hearing at the magistrates' courts, the prosecution papers will be reviewed. These will include: a summary of the case; the charge sheet; prosecution witness statements; the defendant's taped interview; and a list of Jimmy's previous convictions. Jimmy will have a chance to discuss these papers with his solicitor and decide whether he will plead guilty or not guilty. In the courtroom, Jimmy will stand in the dock and be asked to give his name, address and date of birth. He will then be asked if he is ready to enter his plea. In our case study, Jimmy pleads not guilty and is therefore sent to the Crown Court for trial. The prosecutor will then recommend whether Jimmy should be remanded into custody by the court or released on bail, conditionally or unconditionally. His solicitor will then make representations for bail on his behalf. The magistrates will make the final decision about whether Jimmy is bailed or remanded into custody. Jimmy's refusal to submit a guilty plea, along with the degree of violence he exhibited, led the magistrate to be concerned about Jimmy's risk of further offending. His application for bail was refused and he was remanded into custody.

Box 2.6: Classification of cases in England and Wales

Summary-only offences are cases that (almost always) can only be tried in the magistrates' court. By default, the maximum sentence that can be imposed is six months' imprisonment (although many offences have a lower maximum sentence). Examples of summary-only offences include: most driving offences; common assault; and public order offences.

'Triable either way' offences are offences that can be tried either (hence their name) in the magistrates' court or in the Crown Court.

The seriousness of the case may vary considerably in terms of harm caused – from more minor to very serious. Examples of 'triable either way' offences include: theft; actual bodily harm; criminal damage; burglary and possession/possession with intent to supply/supplying drugs; and arson (without endangering life).

Indictable-only offences are generally the most serious offences that can lead to a lengthy term of imprisonment. If someone is charged with such a case, they will initially appear at the magistrates' courts to be sent to the Crown Court for trial/ sentencing. Examples of indictable-only offences are: murder; manslaughter; grievous bodily harm; rape; arson; and robbery.

All trials and sentencing for indictable-only offences are held at the **Crown Court**. Prior to any trial, however, a plea and case management hearing will be held, to prepare for the trial and to fix a date.

If Jimmy had pleaded guilty at this stage, the judge would then move to sentencing, having heard mitigation from the defence (excuses or explanations for Jimmy's behaviour that might result in a lesser sentence). By pleading guilty, Jimmy would also have received a reduction in his sentence of up to one third. The first job at trial is to swear in a jury, who will be responsible for finding Jimmy guilty or not guilty, having heard all the evidence. The prosecuting barrister will then outline their case and call witnesses to provide evidence that supports that case. The defence barrister can cross-examine those witnesses. It is then the defence turn to call their own witnesses, which may include Jimmy. The prosecution are then able to cross-examine those witnesses. The judge will then sum up the evidence for the jury, before they retire to consider their verdict. Once the jury has returned their verdict, the judge will then sentence Jimmy, using sentencing guidelines to guide their decision. In our case study, the judge gives Jimmy a sentence of 10 years.

If a defendant is sentenced to custody (or remanded in custody prior to their trial), they are then the responsibility of **Her Majesty's Prison and Probation Service**. This service, and its officers, should accommodate prisoners securely and safely, and enforce discipline by dealing with prisoners who transgress prison rules and, if necessary, by physically restraining prisoners who are considered to be out of control. The service should also develop good relationships with the prisoners, support those not coping, be sensitive to risks of suicide and self-harm, solve problems and respond to requests for help.

Jimmy will have a number of rights in prison, including:

- *protection from bullying and racial harassment;*
- *being able to get in contact with a solicitor;*
- *healthcare, including support for a mental health condition;*
- *being able to spend between 30 minutes and an hour outside in the open air each day.*

Jimmy is released from prison having served six years of his sentence. Offenders serving less than four years are automatically released at the halfway point of their sentence. Because Jimmy was sentenced to over four years in prison, he has to apply to the Parole Board (see Box 2.7) for a decision as to whether he can be released. The Parole Board will consider what Jimmy has done in prison, such as participation in rehabilitation programmes, education or employment training. It will also review his plans for release and, on this basis, will make a recommendation for his release or continuing imprisonment.

Box 2.7: The Parole Board

The Parole Board manages the early release of prisoners serving fixed-term sentences of four years or more and those who are serving life sentences and indeterminate sentences for public protection. There are around 212 part-time Parole Board members, who deal with an average of 500 cases per week. The *Osborn* ruling by the Supreme Court in 2013 resulted in a significant increase in the work of the Parole Board, when three prisoners successfully appealed for the right to an oral hearing rather than the traditional hearing on 'papers' that the Parole Board used.

The Parole Board makes its decisions based on a risk assessment about whether prisoners can be safely released into the community and, as such, carries responsibilities for potential harm that might be caused by people who reoffend as well as to victims and their families.

Criticisms of the Parole Board tend to centre around three main issues:

- the lack of transparent, systematic risk assessment criteria for decision making, leading to confusion about the basis of decisions;
- concerns about the lack of independence of Board members who are appointed by the Secretary of State for Justice and whose guidance the Board follows;
- whether it is too cautious in decision making, leaving lots of low-risk prisoners in prison when they could be released.

Before release from prison, Jimmy will be given his 'licence', which will explain the conditions of his release. This licence will include seven standard conditions, including rules relating to staying in touch with his supervising officer, and not travelling abroad without permission, as well as any extra conditions that his offender manager judges necessary to enable Jimmy's progress and prevent future trouble. If Jimmy breaks the terms and conditions of his licence, he may be recalled to prison immediately, or receive a warning the first or second time he breaks the conditions of his licence. If Jimmy breaches his licence for a third time, he will be recalled to prison.

Jimmy will serve the remaining four years of his sentence under the supervision of the National Probation Service (NPS). It will be responsible for monitoring his behaviour throughout that time and will have the authority to send Jimmy back to prison to serve the remainder of his 10-year sentence, should he breach the conditions of his licence. Jimmy's probation officer will be responsible for ensuring that Jimmy adheres to those conditions, whatever they might be – for example, by adhering to a curfew or exclusion zone, or by attending a cognitive behaviour programme or a drug and alcohol rehabilitation course. The NPS also provides educational opportunities for offenders. Jimmy's rights at this point in his journey revert to those of any individual in the community – it is not the responsibility of the criminal justice system to provide for any of the social or economic needs he might have on release beyond the establishment of a resettlement plan (see Chapter Seven).

The victim's role in criminal justice proceedings

Over the past two decades, both the government and criminal justice agencies have come to a realisation that victims and witnesses play a crucial role in enabling effective and just criminal proceedings. As a result, a much greater focus on supporting victims and witnesses has developed, which in turn has had a significant impact on the role and responsibilities of criminal justice agencies in relation to victims and witnesses (see Chapter Four). This increased focus on the needs and rights of victims culminated in the 2002 White Paper *Justice for all* (MOJ,

2002), which called for a rebalancing of the criminal justice system in favour of victims, witnesses and communities. The subsequent Domestic Violence, Crime and Victims Act 2004 introduced Codes of Practice, which clearly set out requirements for all criminal justice agencies to meet the needs of victims with whom they come into contact. It also set out the process of complaining about unsatisfactory services. Victims of crime who are called as a witness have specific legal entitlements that are set out in the Victims' Code. These include:

- the right to request special measures in court for vulnerable or intimidated witnesses;
- the right to claim for any expenses incurred as a witness in a criminal trial;
- the right to ask court staff to enter the court building through a separate entrance from the defendant and their family and friends;
- the right to request an interpreter when giving evidence as a witness;
- the right to meet the CPS advocate or representative and to ask them questions about the court process, where possible.

To properly assess the effectiveness of these so called 'victim-centred' policies and practices, however, it is important to ascertain whether criminal justice agents are genuinely committed to aiding the recovery of the victim and helping them as much as possible through the criminal justice process. Alternatively, it might be that such policies and practices are geared towards obtaining crucial witness cooperation and thus are more centred on strengthening the prosecution case than on helping victims. Some argue that the criminal justice system only values victims in their role as witnesses and neglects those victims who do not – or cannot – fulfil that function. Furthermore, in those cases that do come to court, it still must be questioned whether the adversarial courtroom is the best place for the victim to tell their story and to have the harm done to them acknowledged by the court, by the defendant and by society as a whole.

In the case study example, because there is to be a trial in the Crown Court, where Jimmy's victim Steve will appear as a prosecution witness to give evidence (and be cross-examined), Steve should receive ongoing support from the various criminal justice agencies as the case progresses. Prior to the trial, Steve will give his statement to the police about what happened. He will be supported by them and by the CPS, who are obliged to keep him informed of progress in the case and to explain any decisions made by them (see Chapter Seven). Steve should also be given the opportunity to give a Victim Personal Statement (VPS), in which he can outline:

- *whether he wants to be told about the progress of the case;*
- *if he would like extra support (particularly when giving evidence);*
- *whether he feels vulnerable or intimidated;*
- *whether he is worried about the offender getting bail;*
- *how the crime has affected him;*
- *if he feels that racial hostility was part of the motivation for that crime – or if his faith, cultural background or disability caused his victimisation;*
- *whether he wants to claim compensation.*

The VPS is taken by the police and is included in the prosecution papers. It should be read by everyone involved in the case, including Jimmy and his team. Since 2013, victims like Steve are also allowed to read out their VPS in court, or have the prosecution barrister read it out, in order that all parties are made aware of the impact the crime has had on them. Steve can also receive support from a Victim Support worker; Victim Support is an independent charity dedicated to providing support for victims of crime. Steve can also be supported in court by the Witness Service, which provides free, practical and emotional support before, during and after a trial. This service operates in every criminal court in England and Wales and is run by Citizens Advice.

Summary

This chapter provides an outline of the key government departments responsible for the criminal justice system and some comparison data about the expenditure and workforce for the agencies explored in subsequent chapters. The police service is the largest agency in terms of cost and workforce. The smallest is the CPS – although its workloads and position in the criminal justice process belie its relatively small size. Having traced a fictitious individual offender through the intricacies of a case, we now turn to examining each of the agencies in more detail.

Guide to data sources and other online resources

Data used in this chapter is derived from the following sources

- Annual Reports and Accounts for each agency provide data relating to expenditure and workforce and are reported in separate chapters.
- Government Budget Estimates provide comparative expenditure across key areas of public policy: https://www.gov.uk/government/organisations/hm-treasury
- Data relating to diversity in the criminal justice system is collated by ethnicity biennially. The most recent data is *Statistics on race and the criminal justice system* (2014): https://www.gov.uk/government/statistics/race-and-the-criminal-justice-system-2014
- The Ministry of Justice produces quarterly caseload statistics that provide data about sentencing and criminal statistics: https://www.gov.uk/government/collections/criminal-justice-statistics-quarterly
- Information about volunteering opportunities within the criminal justice system can be found in: Prison Reform Trust (2013) *What can I do? Your guide to volunteering and achieving change in the criminal justice system.* www.prisonreformtrust.org.uk/Portals/0/Documents/what%20can%20i%20do.pdf

Other websites of interest

- The Home Office website contains broad policy relating to the police service: https://www.gov.uk/government/organisations/home-office
- The Ministry of Justice website contains access to a wide range of statistics, updates to policy and links to key agencies: https://www.gov.uk/government/organisations/ministry-of-justice
- The Attorney General's Office website can be found at: https://www.gov.uk/government/organisations/attorney-generals-office
- Diversity data relating to women is available from the Ministry of Justice. The most recent data is from 2015: https://www.gov.uk/government/collections/women-and-the-criminal-justice-system
- Lammy Review updates can be found at the official website: https://www.gov.uk/government/organisations/lammy-review
- Further information about the work of the Parole Board can be found at: www.gov.uk/government/organisations/parole-board

Taking it further …

More in-depth reading about the issues raised in this chapter

Bowling, B. and Phillips, C. (2002) *Racism, crime and justice*, Harlow: Pearson Education Limited

College of Policing (2015) *College of Policing analysis: Estimating demand on the police service*. www.college.police.uk/documents/demand_report_21_1_15.pdf

Roberts, J. and Manikis, M. (2013) Victim personal statements in England and Wales: Latest (and last) trends from the Witness and Victim Experience Survey, *Criminology and Criminal Justice*, 13(3), 245-61

Questions to consider from this chapter and your further reading

- What impact do you think a change in Home Secretary or Minister of Justice might have on criminal justice policy?
- Why do you think the police account for more than three-quarters of criminal justice expenditure?
- Does the disproportionality reflected in the statistics from the Lammy Review suggest that the criminal justice system is racist?
- Will victims reading out their VPS aloud in court make a difference to levels of victim satisfaction?

THREE

The police service

Background

Since the inception of the 'new' police in 1829, there has been debate and controversy about what the police do, how they do it and how to resolve what appear to be a raft of long-standing issues with the management and accountability of both the service and its officers. This chapter focuses on a 'narrow' view of the police service as an institution and its role within the criminal justice system. However, it is important to acknowledge that 'policing' as an activity encompasses a much broader set of agencies than the Home Office constabularies, including forces with specific remits such as the British Transport Police, Civil Nuclear Constabulary and Ministry of Defence Police, as well as a raft of policing functions carried out by private security firms.

Explaining and understanding why the new police were deemed a necessary development in the early decades of the 19th century is itself open to debate. Most commentators agree that the motivation to establish the Metropolitan Police Service (MPS) was driven by social, economic and political factors that underpinned increasing concern about crime and criminality – particularly among the new urban poor of Victorian England. Historical debates about how and why the new police were founded also indicate that the very establishment of the police service was not without opposition, most notably from those who believed that the new uniformed officers represented a political force to suppress the working classes, particularly in relation to the threat of riots and unrest in urban areas. For others, the establishment of the new police was a rational development that sought to improve the ad-hoc methods of the 'nightwatch' that had existed in some form or another since the 18th century. Certainly, the original aims of the new police articulated a relatively uncontroversial view of their remit – to prevent crime and disorder, although as we shall see the formal aims of the police service tell us little about 'how' those objectives are interpreted and delivered on the ground.

Despite controversy and opposition, there is general agreement that through the first half of the 20th century, the police were able to gain the consent and legitimacy of the population so that the 1950s are often described as the 'heyday' of British policing. In part, this legitimacy stemmed from a core principle of the model adopted (developed) by early policing pioneers based on 'policing by consent' – namely that the police rely on the support of the public in the exercise of their duties rather than the application of force (see Box 3.1).

However, the 'heyday' of the 1950s has not been maintained. Controversy after controversy dogged the police service throughout the 20th century, culminating in official inquiries, Royal Commissions, changes to legislation and numerous reviews and critical debates that provide the immediate context to the remainder of this discussion. The central message from reading the history of policing is that very little that police officers do is without controversy or opposition, but their very existence remains unquestioned. On the basis that the police, therefore, perform an undisputed role in criminal justice, this chapter first provides an overview of how the service is organised and the key powers of police officers. The discussion then moves on to outline key issues and debates that frame the way the police are viewed by the

1829 Metropolitan Police Improvement Act ⬤ **1856** County and Boroughs Police Act ⬤

public and commentators – namely, accountability, corruption and malpractice and the culture of the police. The chapter ends with a focus on the relationship between the police and minority ethnic groups.

Box 3.1: Features of consensual and military models of policing

Policing by consent	Military models of policing
Emphasises due process/human rights and the transparency of law enforcement	Use of covert methods of surveillance and 'spies' is tolerated
A focus on community safety, including preventing crime	Focus is 'fighting crime'
Independent of political control and non-partisan	Controlled by government and elites
Principle of minimal use of force against citizens means officers are not routinely armed	Officers are routinely armed and use of weapons is tolerated
Order is maintained through negotiation	Order is maintained through force

1856 Establishment of HM Inspectorate of Constabulary ◠ **1878** Criminal Investigation Department of the Metropolitan Police established ◠

Organisation and delivery

There is no single national police service for the United Kingdom. Instead, policing is organised around 'territorial' police forces that are responsible for the policing of specific local authority or geographical areas. In England and Wales there are 43 operational police forces, working across 174 local authority areas. Northern Ireland is served by a single force, The Police Service of Northern Ireland (PSNI) (established in 2001), as is Scotland – Police Scotland (since 2013).

Typically, each force will comprise a number of basic command units that split the larger force area into smaller territorial units. These local units are responsible for delivering frontline policing to local communities and are served by central support functions and specialist units that operate force-wide. There is no standard size for local policing units either in terms of the size of population served or the number of officers, which ostensibly allows them to be organised around local priorities and needs. Each force is managed by a Chief Constable, who is responsible for the operational delivery of all policing functions, supported by a management team that usually comprises senior police officers and a number of civilian specialists (in financial management, for example).

However, there are limitations to the localised structure of policing, particularly in relation to organised crime, that demand more centralised approaches. Various iterations of this have existed since the establishment of Regional Crime Squads in the 1960s. Today, the National Crime Agency provides policing support across a range of organised crime activities, including child sexual exploitation, cyber crime and organised immigration crime (see Box 3.2).

Box 3.2: The role of the National Crime Agency

The National Crime Agency was established in 2013, the third 'national' agency in 15 years to be tasked with dealing with organised and cross-border crime. The NCA's remit goes wider than that of its predecessors, in having the power to instruct other police forces and agencies to carry out specific tasks – powers that have seen it nicknamed 'the British FBI'. Unlike its North American counterpart, however, it does not have responsibility for terrorism, which remains under the remit of the Metropolitan Police. NCA officers number around 4,000 and operate across 40 countries. To assist them in their wide-ranging duties, they are 'triple warranted': holding the powers of a constable, immigration officer and customs officer.

The police are unique among criminal justice agencies for receiving income from local *and* national government. The major proportion of police funding comes from the Home Office. A funding formula is used to calculate how much each force should receive and this is given to the police and crime commissioners (PCCs) (or equivalents) to allocate across police functions in their area. In addition to the Home Office grant, local authorities collect a 'precept' through council tax paid by households, and this is also given to PCCs to allocate.

According to the National Audit Office (2015), central grant funding to police forces decreased by 25% in real terms (taking account of inflation) for the period 2010-11 to 2015-16, amounting to a reduction of £2.3 billion (see Figure 3.1). All forces are able to counteract the effect of these cuts through increases in council tax precept – in fact, the average total funding reduction for all forces was 18%, once all income was taken into account. However, depending on how reliant forces are on central funding, some feel the pain more than others.

1974 Introduction of Police National Computer ● **1976** Police Act ●

Figure 3.1: Central government revenue funding for the police, 2010-11 to 2015-16

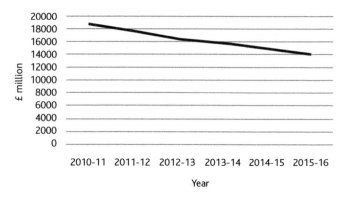

A briefing paper for the House of Commons Library on Police Funding (see Johnston and Politowski, 2016) explains the variations in more detail. For example, in Surrey Police, the Home Office grant makes up 51% of total funding, with the remaining 49% coming from council tax precept, and therefore the effect of central government reductions is less severe – in reality, Surrey saw a 12% decrease in funding between 2010-11 and 2015-16 compared to the average of 18%. In contrast, Northumbria's overall funding reduction was 23%, because the Home Office grant makes up 88% of police funding here, and so the effects of central government cuts are felt more acutely.

During the same period, the numbers of police officers has fallen – from 139,110 in 2010-11 to 124,066 in 2015-16 and thus austerity has led to an overall reduction in officer capacity (see Table 3.1). However, police officer numbers have not fallen as sharply as those in other areas of the workforce, in particular the number of police community support officers (PCSOs), whose strength has fallen by 43.3% since 2010-11 (see Box 3.3 for definitions of staff groupings).

Table 3.1: Police service workforce numbers by type, March 2011 to March 2016

Work type	March 2011	March 2012	March 2013	March 2014	March 2015	March 2016	% change from 2011
Police officers	139,110	134,100	129,584	127,909	127,192	124,066	-12.1
Police staff	74,010	67,472	65,509	64,097	63,894	61,668	-20.0
PCSOs	15,820	14,393	14,205	13,066	12,370	11,043	-43.3
Designated officers	4,064	4,120	4,314	4,273	4,254	4,130	1.6
Traffic wardens	252	36	21	16	18	15	-
Special constables	18,421	20,343	19,011	17,764	16,074	15,996	-15.2
Total	251,677	240,464	232,644	227,125	223,802	216,918	-16.0

Source: Police workforce statistics 2011 to 2016 (Home Office; available online: https://www.gov.uk/government/collections/police-workforce-england-and-wales)

Total workforce data for the police belies significant differences across forces, however. The MPS employs a quarter of all officers (25.9%) and almost half of all officers (48.3%) are employed by just eight forces (MPS, City of London, Greater Manchester, Merseyside, Northumbria, South Yorkshire, West Midlands and West Yorkshire).

Box 3.3: Employee groups in the police service

- **Police officers** – this term is applied to employees who have taken an oath to uphold the law. Police officers can draw on the full range of police powers in pursuit of their duties.
- **Police staff** – this category refers to all service employees, other than police officers and designated officers.
- **Police community support officers** – a specific type of designated officer, employed in a highly visible patrolling role. They have limited powers available to them in pursuit of their duties.
- **Designated officers** – staff who are not police officers, who can exercise specific powers that would otherwise be available to police officers to fulfil specific roles: PCSO, investigation officer, detention officer and escort officer.
- **Special constables** – part-time volunteer officers, who have all the same powers as regular police officers.

Box 3.3 describes the five distinct employee groupings within the police service. These employee groups indicate changes in the police workforce that have arisen since the 1980s. In response to the new public management agenda, police forces have been encouraged to focus on 'core' functions. This has led to many activities being passed to a civilian workforce (police staff), as well as the contracting out of some activities to private sector companies. The introduction of PCSOs in 2002 increased the number of people on 'patrol', providing a visible reassurance presence without the need to employ additional officers, while designated officers are given limited powers to fulfil some roles (including custody officer). 'Special' constables are volunteers who work alongside the police and perform many of the same functions as police officers.

1994 Police and Magistrates Courts Act ⟳ **1999** Macpherson Report published ⟳

Police workforce data for March 2016 also shows that the overwhelming majority of police officers are white (94.1%) and male (71.4%). This lack of representativeness across the police service has been of concern to many who argue that this lack of diversity undermines police legitimacy. (The 'Focus on ...' section at the end of this chapter takes a closer look at the issue of race in the police service.)

Police workloads can be calculated across numerous variables, including public calls for assistance (14 million in 2016) and 999 emergency calls (8 million in 2016), many of which are not crime related, reflecting one function of the police as an emergency service. With regard to their role in the criminal justice system, however, the focus here is on the number of suspects arrested. Figure 3.2 shows the trends in arrest since 2010-11, which have seen overall reductions of 51%.

Figure 3.2: Total arrests, 2010-11 to 2015-16

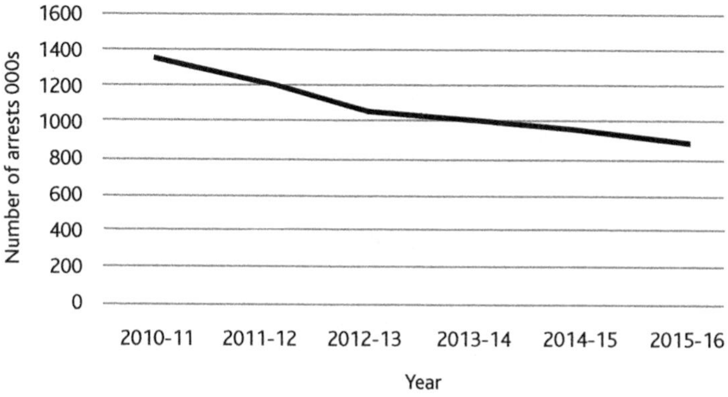

Number of arrests 000s

Year

Functions and powers

It is a fairly well rehearsed statement in most criminology textbooks that very little of what the police 'do' is actually related to crime.

Instead, the functions of the police are expressed as a wide-ranging set of activities that can include almost anything from investigating crime to providing security for a state visit (see Box 3.4)

Box 3.4: Functions of police officers

- **Public reassurance** – visible patrol and community engagement.
- **Crime reduction** – use of visible patrol and public communication.
- **Crime investigation** – identify and arrest offenders and bring them to justice.
- **Emergency service** – rapid response to accidents, emergencies and disturbances.
- **Peace keeping** – negotiation and problem solving in neighbourhood disputes and disorder.
- **Order maintenance** – controlling crowds at public events, such as sporting events and demonstrations.
- **State security** – including the protection of public figures and state buildings, as well as covert policing of dissident organisations.

The functions of the police service are further complicated by the myriad models of police practice that might be employed to tackle crime. Some examples of these different styles of policing are shown in Box 3.5 – each of them require different levels of resource and training, produce different outcomes and are frequently employed in tandem to tackle different types of crime.

2002 Police Reform Act 🔵 **2010** Crime and Security Act 🔵

Box 3.5: Examples of styles of policing

- **Community-oriented policing** – involvement of local communities in priority setting; close relationships between police officers and local communities; use of visible foot patrols ('bobbies on the beat') rather than vehicles.
- **Problem-oriented policing (POP)** – application of scientific analysis methods to gather information about crime, set priorities and develop tailor-made responses.
- **Intelligence-led policing** – shares features of the POP model, but includes proactive gathering of intelligence through covert methods alongside data analysis.
- **Restorative policing** – involves community and individuals in informal sanctioning, going further than community policing; requires careful negotiation and management of parties to avoid conflict.

Additional complexity in police function arises from the potential for competing priorities to affect day-to-day operations: for example, a national crime priority to deal with anti-social behaviour could compete with local community priorities to prevent crime through improving relations with young people. On the one hand, the police are being asked to increase the rates of arrest or prosecution for a criminal offence that is generating public concern; while on the other hand, they are trying to build positive relationships with those who are most likely to be involved in committing these kinds of offences.

Despite this operational fuzziness, in terms of the criminal justice system the police play a crucial role as 'gatekeepers': they decide which crimes are investigated, who is arrested and collect the evidence upon which subsequent prosecution might be based. As such, they

2011 Police Reform and Social Responsibility Act 🔁 **2012** First Police Crime Commissioner Elections 🔁

are provided with a range of powers that are unique to their status as officers of the law.

Thus, the police play a crucial role in defining the way that crime is responded to in society generally, and who is defined as a 'criminal' – but they do not do so with total freedom. The introduction of the Police and Criminal Evidence Act (known as PACE) in 1984 established a codified framework that is designed to protect suspects and give the police sufficient power to investigate cases with a view to successful prosecution (see Box 3.6).

Box 3.6: Police Powers under PACE (1984) and relevant Codes of Practice

- Part I – Powers to stop and search (Code A)
- Part II – Powers of entry, search and seizure (Code B)
- Part III – Powers of arrest (Code G)
- Part IV – Power to detain (Code C)
- Part V – Questioning and treatment of suspects by the police (Code C).

Additional Codes of Practice cover:

- Code D – Methods of identification
- Code E – Audio recording
- Code F – Visual recording.

The balance between successful outcomes for the police (securing evidence to win the case) and protecting the rights of suspects lies at the heart of debates about the operation of PACE in practice. The following three examples highlight some of the tensions that run throughout the criminal justice system in this regard: powers to stop and search and 'reasonable suspicion'; changes to powers of arrest; and rights of suspects who are detained.

Stop and Search

Section I of PACE allows an officer to stop and search (a person or vehicle) if they have reasonable grounds for suspecting that they will find stolen or prohibited articles or offensive weapons. It is the inclusion of the phrase 'reasonable grounds' that causes the most controversy in this case, because although the Code of Practice indicates that this should not be a decision made on the grounds of personal appearance, it is widely held that the discretion this affords police officers can give rise to discrimination (see the 'Focus on ... ' section at the end of this chapter).

Arrest

Historically, the police needed permission from a magistrate (a warrant) to arrest someone suspected of any offence except the most serious. However, since the Serious Organised Crime and Police Act 2005, the distinction between 'arrestable' (more serious) and non-arrestable (less serious) offences no longer exists. This has raised concerns by some commentators about the potential threat this may cause to individual liberties, where a person could be arrested (and therefore detained) for a relatively minor offence simply to facilitate questioning by the police. These arguments raise important questions about the relationship between the police and civilians and do little to protect individuals from police power to detain, even for minor offences.

Detention

Some of the more visible changes to police practice introduced by PACE related to the introduction of specific rights for suspects when in detention at the police station. PACE saw the introduction of 'custody officers', whose role it is to guarantee these rights and to ensure the welfare of those in detention (see Chapter Two). However, although these rights exist and suspects may be told about them, it does not necessarily follow that individuals will be in a position to understand their rights or take advantage of them.

Protecting 'vulnerable' suspects

In light of these difficulties, special measures are provided for 'vulnerable' suspects, a category that includes young people, those with mental health problems or learning disabilities, and those who are hearing impaired. In these instances, the police are not supposed to question suspects without the presence of an appropriate adult – who is often a social worker but might also be a parent or a volunteer – who can ensure that suspects' rights are protected and provide advice. Given that the police routinely interact with those with vulnerabilities, the success of the appropriate adult scheme might be taken as a measure of the extent to which the police place any importance on whether suspects' rights are preserved. The National Appropriate Adult Network estimates that between 11% and 22% of detainees could meet the threshold for needing an appropriate adult but that rates of identification among police forces average 3.1%, which suggests a significant under-identification of need by the police.

Key debates

Selecting those issues that are central to understanding some of the debates that occur with regard to policing is fraught with difficulty, since the wide range of activities they undertake may all deserve consideration, notwithstanding wider debates relating to police powers and use of force, for example. Here, the focus is on three themes that bring together a range of more specific questions about the police and point to some of the difficulties that might exist in seeking to reform this somewhat symbolic institution as follows:

- **Accountability** – who should control the police? What is the role of the public in holding the police accountable for their actions? How independent should the police service be?
- **Corruption and malpractice** – what might constitute wrongdoing by a police officer? Is it possible to eliminate corruption and malpractice in a job that brings police officers into routine contact with criminals and gives them high levels of discretion?
- **Police culture** – what are the characteristics of police culture? How might police culture impede capacity for reform within the service?

Accountability

The police are widely researched and inspected with myriad scrutiny on their activities provided by inspectorate reports, the Public Accounts Committee, Home Office data collection requirements, and so on. This scrutiny has not happened by accident – there are good reasons why maintaining oversight of police activity is important, not least the reality that they act as gatekeepers to the criminal justice system and are empowered to detain and interrogate members of the public. This scrutiny is particularly relevant to the application of police powers and the way in which PACE provides a system of checks and balances to hold police officers to account through the courts, for example. As well as this legal framework for accountability, individual police officers can be held to account through the complaints system (see Box 3.7).

Box 3.7: The Independent Police Complaints Commission (IPCC)

The IPCC dates from 2004, and was established through the Police Reform Act 2002 to replace the Police Complaints Authority. The IPCC oversees the police complaints system in England and Wales and investigates all serious cases, regardless of whether there is a complaint, that involve police officers. Examples of serious cases include those involving the use of firearms or deaths in custody. The IPCC can: investigate cases independently; supervise the force investigation; or pass back to the police for local investigation. In reality, only the most serious cases remain under independent investigation. The IPCC also considers appeals from people who are dissatisfied with the way their complaint has been dealt with at force level.

Of particular importance is how the police are accountable to the communities they serve – the principle of policing by consent has consistently held that what the police 'do' should align with the public's wishes. Central to this has been the so-called 'tri-partite system' of governance established by the Police Act 1964, which set up a structure of governance for the police that still holds today. Rather than a simple top-down model of governance leading from government to chief constables, the 'tri-partite' structure was intended to ensure that there was a balance of power between central government (through the Home Secretary), operational policing (chief constables) and the public (historically a local police authority, but now through Police and Crime Panels).

In 2012, the Police Reform and Social Responsibility Act introduced a fourth element to the structure – Police and Crime Commissioners (PCCs), who are elected every four years. PCCs are responsible for police budgets and for setting police and crime priorities through a local crime plan. They can also hold chief constables to account and have the power to remove a chief constable from office. Oversight of PCCs is provided by Police and Crime Panels, made up of 10 local councillors and two lay members – effectively replacing the police authorities that had previously provided the 'public' element of the tripartite system.

In terms of accountability, the arguments in favour of PCCs is that they allow the public, through the election process, to have a greater say in how crime is dealt with in their area. However, the legitimacy of PCCs in this role is somewhat undermined by low turnouts in elections (just 15% in the first elections in 2014) and the dominance of candidates from major political parties, which raised questions about whether the police could maintain its political independence.

Corruption and malpractice

For every TV drama that portrays the solid and dependable police officer who is trustworthy and honest, there are equal numbers of stories of police officers who accept bribes, tamper with evidence, or undermine criminal investigations by committing perjury or physical abuse of suspects. The reality is that corruption is generally held to be a problem that affects all police forces anywhere in the world – one that is not bounded by rank or department. However, defining police corruption is notoriously difficult and can include a range of actions that might appear fairly innocuous, such as the acceptance of gratuities, and hence it is increasingly viewed as an ethical issue. Her Majesty's Inspectorate of Constabulary and Fire & Rescue Services (HMICFRS) identifies a range of behaviours that it views 'of concern' when considering police corruption (HMIC, 2015):

- drug-related offences
- bribery
- theft, including fraud and dishonesty

- sexual misconduct
- unauthorised information disclosure
- inappropriate relationships with the media
- incompatible business interests or other jobs
- racial discrimination
- other types of discrimination.

Explaining the causes of corruption is similarly complex – the idea that corruption is restricted to a few 'bad apples' is generally accepted to be incompatible with the evidence of widespread 'institutional' levels of wrongdoing. However, many of the causes of corruption lie within the nature of policing itself – the view that there is an inherent potential for corruption to always exist, because of the complex decisions that police officers are asked to make and the levels of discretion they are afforded in doing so. Some of these features are 'constant' – they are always present in policing – while others are variable and might indicate the context within which specific examples of corruption occur (see Box 3.8).

Box 3.8: Features of policing that increase likelihood of corruption

Constant features:

- discretion
- low managerial and public visibility
- peer group secrecy
- association with criminals.

Variable features:

- tolerance of corruption in community and politics
- organisational integrity and control

- contact with opportunities for corruption (working in particular areas such as vice)
- degrees of accountability
- degree of moral cynicism among officers.

(Adapted from Newburn, 2015)

Against a backdrop of complexity around both the definition and cause of corruption, it is hardly any wonder that dealing with wrongdoing by police officers is also fraught with difficulty. Alongside professional standards that might be undermined by misconduct, police officers are also accountable to the law and potentially face criminal charges for corruption. However, the ambiguity surrounding the definition and cause of corruption makes consistent punishment problematic, and variations in the way different forces deal with allegations further complicate the process.

In an attempt to promote a more positive spin on the issue, the College of Policing developed a 'Code of Ethics' that is intended to provide a framework for 'good' policing instead of a focus on managing misconduct (see Box 3.9).

Box 3.9: Standards of professional behaviour for police officers

1.   Honesty and Integrity – I will be honest and act with integrity at all times, and will not compromise or abuse my position.
2.   Authority, respect and courtesy – I will act with self-control and tolerance, treating members of the public and colleagues with respect and courtesy. I will use my powers and authority lawfully and proportionately, and will respect the rights of all individuals.

3. Equality and diversity – I will act with fairness and impartiality. I will not discriminate unlawfully or unfairly.

4. Use of force – I will only use force as part of my role and responsibilities, and only to the extent that it is necessary, proportionate and reasonable in all the circumstances.

5. Orders and instructions – I will, as a police officer, give and carry out lawful orders only, and will abide by Police Regulations. I will give reasonable instructions only, and will follow all reasonable instructions.

6. Duties and responsibilities – I will be diligent in the exercise of my duties and responsibilities.

7. Confidentiality – I will treat information with respect, and access or disclose it only in the proper course of my duties.

8. Fitness for work – I will ensure, when on duty or at work, that I am fit to carry out my responsibilities.

9. Conduct – I will behave in a manner, whether on or off duty, which does not bring discredit on the police service or undermine public confidence in policing.

10. Challenging and reporting improper behaviour – I will report, challenge or take action against the conduct of colleagues which has fallen below the standards of professional behaviour.

Source: College of Policing (2014)

Thus, a focus on the ethics of policing avoids complex definitions of what corrupt behaviour might be and why it might occur, and gives a framework for interpreting all forms of police actions.

'Cop culture'

One of the most enduring ways of trying to understand police behaviour has been the idea of 'cop culture'. The term describes a shared set of values, attitudes and beliefs that define the way police officers understand their role and subsequently pervade their everyday interactions with the public and each other. It is argued that cop culture is passed down from experienced officers to new recruits through a process of socialisation, or learning 'how to be' a police officer. Socialisation happens in almost all occupational settings, but is particularly important in police work, where learning how to exercise discretion becomes part of the tacit knowledge that new recruits might learn once they have completed their initial training. If the imparting of that tacit knowledge includes socialisation into unethical or negative characteristics, then logic dictates that unless the very nature of police work changes, the culture will simply continue to be recycled.

Box 3.10 describes the seven characteristics of cop culture made famous by Robert Reiner's (2010) analysis of the research in the field.

Box 3.10: Seven characteristics of cop culture

- **Mission (action-cynicism-pessimism):** Police work as a mission to preserve order that involves 'fighting crime'. In undertaking this mission, police officers can become cynical about human behaviour and only see the negative in this.
- **Suspicion:** In order to be effective, police officers are necessarily suspicious. This is reinforced by the danger inherent in some elements of policing.
- **Isolation/solidarity:** Shift work and other traits such as suspicion can leave police officers feeling isolated, which generates strong bonds between colleagues, and an 'us' and 'them' mentality that separates them from other social groups.
- **Conservatism:** A moral conservatism that underpins a sense of mission and a strong sense of maintaining things 'as they are'.

- ■ **Machismo:** Valuing particular attributes such as physical strength, bravery and sexual promiscuity that are associated with a hyper-masculinity that generates negative perceptions of women.
- ■ **Racial prejudice:** May emanate from the nature of police work and 'them and us' attitudes that generate prejudicial attitudes, but studies have repeatedly identified racial prejudice in the police working personality.
- ■ **Pragmatism:** Also generated by the nature of the work, police officers tend to be 'down to earth' rather than progressive in their attitudes.

Adapted from Reiner (2010).

These characteristics can be used to explain a variety of less-than-positive police practices, including the failure of the police service to address racism; attitudes towards certain types of crime such as rape or domestic violence; the collusion of officers in corruption or malpractice investigations, and so on. However, many of the traits associated with cop culture are also positive: teamwork and camaraderie can provide support to officers in times of stress as well as encouraging bravery in times of danger.

Much of Reiner's analysis is based on relatively old research from the UK and the US. More recent scholars have been critical of the cop culture model, raising important questions about the resonance of these characteristics in contemporary policing. Four of the more important criticisms raised are as follows.First, what the police 'do' is not the same as what they 'say' they do. Drawing attention to the existence of a 'canteen culture', where storytelling and bravado might be more important than reflecting the reality of policing, commentators point to the importance of separating out how police officers behave when on duty with the kinds of attitudes they might exhibit in private.

Second, it is inadequate to present a single monolithic police culture as if all officers think or behave in the same way. Instead, we need to be more nuanced in our understanding of a multiplicity of 'cultures' within the police, depending on the type of work individuals do including specific 'management cop' culture and 'detective' cultures. Accordingly, we might think of Reiner's 2010 analysis as a description of 'street cop' culture rather than other types of culture. Furthermore, as policing becomes more diverse – more women, more officers from minority ethnic groups and more graduate entrants – the likelihood of a single culture existing or persisting seems absurd.

Third, cop culture models present recruits as if they were simply empty vessels, who bring no individual agency or personal values to the job. This is an important issue to reflect upon, particularly in the context of seeking to change police behaviour or attitudes. Some elements of the cop culture model assume that this is a 'learned' process by recruits, but that is not necessarily the case, since it is also feasible that people who apply to serve as a police officer already share these attitudes and beliefs and that is why they are drawn to the service. This argument was more powerful when the majority of officers were recruited from white, male, working-class backgrounds and so cop culture could be seen as simply reflecting those prevailing societal values. This argument is less powerful when recruitment is more diverse and individuals with widely different attitudes and values might become part of the service. In this scenario, the capacity for individual agency and diverse values to influence aspects of police work are more positive, and the assumption that all recruits will be 'duped' into cop culture is less persuasive.

Fourth, and finally, there are those critics who suggest that the emphasis placed on cop culture occurs at the expense of the social, political and organisational context within which policing takes place. These arguments draw attention to the importance of seeing the police service as part of a wider state and social enterprise that both reflects and creates responses to criminal behaviour based on prevailing societal values. This perspective emphasises more positive potential for external pressure (whether from government, society or the media) to generate change within the service.

Despite these criticisms, and some debate about the extent to which any or all of these characteristics dominate any or all of the different parts of the police service, the literature on police culture has been hugely influential, in drawing attention to the ways in which the institution might perpetuate particular attitudes, and why it remains impervious to efforts to reform police officer behaviour.

Focus on ... policing black and minority ethnic groups

The figures presented in Chapter Two showed that there is disproportionality with regard to black and minority ethnic (BAME) groups throughout the criminal justice system, and we discussed the ways in which this might be interpreted as evidence of discrimination operating throughout the system, in part as a result of the high levels of discretion afforded to criminal justice practitioners. Nowhere are these debates more hotly contested or documented than with regard to police–BAME relations, which can be traced back to at least the 1970s, if not before, and which have given rise to some of the most widely cited official reports and inquiries, including the Scarman Report (1981) and the Macpherson Report (1999).

The Scarman Report (1981) followed riots in Brixton in 1981 that arose from 'Operation Swamp', where police officers were instructed to stop and search as many people as possible over a week-long period. Over half the people stopped were black and two-thirds were under the age of 21. Scarman was critical of the heavy-handed nature of the operation, which exacerbated already strained relations between the police and the community. The reforms that Scarman recommended included: better training of officers in diversity issues; the use of community policing models; and changes to stop and search powers.

The Macpherson Inquiry almost two decades later into the circumstances surrounding the death of Stephen Lawrence and the failures of the subsequent police investigation similarly identified the use of stop and search as one of the critical problems underpinning poor police–BAME relations (see Box 3.11). The report made 70 recommendations across a wide range of police practices, including victim liaison, the management of murder investigations and, most importantly, the need to improve trust and confidence of BAME communities in the police.

Box 3.11: The Macpherson Inquiry and institutional racism

In April 1993, black teenager Stephen Lawrence was stabbed to death in what was ultimately accepted to be a racially motivated attack by a gang of white youths. At the time, no-one was successfully charged with the murder and the police were widely criticised for their handling of the case, including the treatment of Stephen's parents and his friend Duwayne Brooks, who had been with Stephen at the time of the murder. In 1997, the newly elected Labour government launched an independent inquiry into the matters arising from Stephen's death and the Macpherson report was published in 1999. The inquiry found that the police investigation was:

'marred by a combination of professional incompetence, institutional racism and a failure of leadership by senior officers' (Macpherson, 1999, paragraph 46.1).

It defined institutional racism as:

The collective failure of an organisation to provide an appropriate and professional service to people because of their colour, culture or ethnic origin. It can be seen or detected in processes, attitudes and behaviour which amount to discrimination through unwitting prejudice, ignorance, thoughtlessness, and racist stereotyping which disadvantage minority ethnic people (Macpherson, 1999, paragraph 6.4)

While some have argued that the focus Macpherson placed on race in his report undermined other aspects of incompetency demonstrated by the police investigation that deserved more widespread attention, there is little doubt that the impact of Macpherson on the police service was immediate and wide-ranging, including the establishment of the IPCC and, for some at least, changing the 'climate' of policing.

After a protracted legal battle that necessitated changes in the law on double jeopardy, two men were eventually convicted of Stephen's murder in 2012. They received custodial sentences of 15 years.

In both the Scarman and Macpherson reports, concerns were raised about the use of stop and search powers by the police against BAME groups as well as the importance of increasing the number of BAME officers within the police service as a mechanism for improving community relations and increasing police legitimacy in the eyes of BAME communities. The discussion that follows focuses on these two issues in more detail.

The most frequently cited data relating to police—ethnic minority relations is 'stop and search'. The data for 2016 shows that those from BAME groups were three times more likely to be stopped and searched than their white counterparts and that although the number of stops has fallen overall, they have fallen most for white individuals. Table 3.2

shows the proportion of all stop and search by ethnicity for 2010-11 and 2015-16. There are a number of observations that can be made from the data presented:

Table 3.2: Proportion of stop and search by self-defined ethnicity, 2010-11 and 2015-16

	2010-11				2015-16			
	White	Black/ Black British	Asian/ Asian British	Chinese and Other	White	Black/ Black British	Asian/ Asian British	Chinese and Other
All excluding Metropolitan Police Service	83.1	4.1	6.3	0.5	76	6	7	1
Metropolitan Police Service	42.0	30.7	16.3	2.5	41	30	13	2
All	64.4	16.3	10.8	1.4	62	16	10	1

Source: Police Powers and Procedures, England and Wales, March 2011 and March 2016

- ▪ First, that outside of the MPS (London), stop and search does not reflect disproportionality overall. Within the capital, however, significant disproportionality occurs for all BAME groups.
- ▪ Second, that overall there has not been very much progress in shifting this disproportionality since 2010. This kind of evidence presents the case for disproportionality in policing and is frequently used to argue that it highlights the way in which frontline police officers use racial stereotypes when exercising their powers.

However, there has been controversy about the way stop and search data are represented. The argument here is that rates of stop and search are presented per 1,000 of the *resident* population (that is the population who live in a particular area) rather than the *available* population (that is the population using public spaces where the police patrol) and that if available population estimates are used, rates of stop and search are the same for BAME and white groups. These findings suggest that racial stereotyping by frontline police officers may not be generating discriminatory outcomes after all, but instead raise questions about managerial decision making about 'where' police officers patrol and therefore 'who' the available population at any given time might be.

Regardless of the problems with data collection and presentation, it is still the case that perceptions of disproportionality among BAME communities persist and that it continues to be a source of tension. The impact of this should not be underestimated, because tension can turn into disturbance – high-profile riots over the last five decades are testament to the ill-feeling that bubbles under the surface in those places that are *over policed and under protected*.

Both Scarman and Macpherson identified the importance of increasing recruitment from among BAME groups as a key element in improving community relations. Police workforce statistics show that the proportion of BAME officers has indeed increased from 3.6% in 2006 to 5.9% in March 2016. Despite these increases, the proportion of BAME officers still falls significantly short of representativeness of the population, where 14% are from BAME groups. The MPS has the highest proportion of BAME officers at 12.6%, but London also has the largest proportion of BAME population at 40.2% – suggesting that even those forces that are relatively successful with BAME recruitment are still unable to achieve representativeness more broadly. It is also the case that the police service has been unable to make inroads into diversifying the workforce across ethnic groups with higher proportions of Asian/Asian British officers (39.9%) compared to Black/Black British (29%) or Chinese (11.2%).

While overall officer numbers give an indication of improving recruitment, they reveal little about the retention and promotion of

BAME officers, which is an important element in diversification of the workforce. Among senior ranks, just 1.1% of police officers are BAME, and workforce data shows that BAME officers are more likely to leave the force because of dismissal or voluntary resignation than white officers.

The evidence suggests that despite improvements, the police service seems impervious to reform – although officer numbers have risen, they remain woefully short of representative and poor retention rates suggest that even when the police are successful in recruiting black officers, they are not good at providing a conducive working environment.

It is unsurprising that politicians have been critical of these efforts. The House of Commons Home Affairs Committee (2016), for example, has called for more proactive action to be taken to improve BAME diversity. It recommends: compulsory training on diversity issues for selection and promotion panel members; increased use of external assessors from a BAME background on selection panels; instituting coaching and mentoring for BAME officers; and ensuring that units which deal with complaints from officers on personnel matters receive dedicated training on diversity issues.

This necessarily brief focus on policing BAME communities serves to highlight the complexity in understanding how the criminal justice system measures and responds to accusations of discrimination, disproportionality and inequality. There is little doubt that official reports have identified clear problems with the policing of BAME communities, and the promotion of anti-discriminatory practice should be a welcome shift away from assumptions that equal treatment is adequate to deal with entrenched attitudes. Problems remain, however – particularly with recruitment and retention and promotion of BAME officers, without which the principle that BAME communities are policed 'by consent' remains an unrealistic proposition.

Summary

- The 'new' police were established in 1829, based on a policing by consent model that prioritises the principle that what the police do should align with citizens' wishes.
- There is no national police service in England and Wales. Instead, each of the 43 separate forces operates independently under the direction of a Chief Constable and an elected police and crime commissioner.
- The police are the gatekeepers to the criminal justice system – they decide who to arrest and are responsible for the collection of evidence in criminal prosecutions.
- Consistency in the application of police powers is formally provided through the Police and Criminal Evidence Act 1984 (PACE), but police officers have considerable discretion in the application of these powers at street level.
- The introduction of police and crime commissioners in 2012 has raised questions about the ongoing political independence of the police and the degree to which they remain accountable to the public.
- The potential for corruption in any police service is high, especially given the wide-ranging powers and discretion they can exercise. Increasingly, corruption and malpractice are addressed as ethical issues and the Code of Ethics for police officers seeks to promote positive behaviour rather than focusing on discipline.
- The existence of a 'cop culture' is often viewed as a barrier to changing police officer attitudes, but is difficult to break down given the nature of police work.

Guide to data sources and other online resources

Data used in this chapter is derived from the following sources

- ■ Police workforce, England and Wales statistics (Home Office): https://www.gov.uk/government/collections/police-workforce-england-and-wales
- ■ Police Powers and Procedures, England and Wales (Home Office) – includes data on arrest, stop and search and other PACE powers: https://www.gov.uk/government/collections/police-powers-and-procedures-england-and-wales
- ■ PEEL Assessment Data from HMICFRS contains detailed information about each force across Effectiveness and Efficiency, including open data tables that can be interrogated for specific information: https://www.justiceinspectorates.gov.uk/hmicfrs/our-work/peel-assessments

Other websites of interest

- ■ Independent Police Complaints Commission: https://www.ipcc.gov.uk
- ■ College of Policing: www.college.police.uk

All local forces also have their own dedicated web pages, as do police and crime commissioners.

Taking it further ...

More in-depth reading about the issues raised in this chapter

Bowling, B. and Phillips, C. (2007) Disproportionate and discriminatory: Reviewing the evidence on police stop and search, *The Modern Law Review*, 70(6), 936-61

Cockcroft, T. (2013) *Police culture: Themes and concepts*, London: Routledge

Punch, M. (2009) *Police corruption: Deviance, accountability and reform in policing*, Cullompton: Willan

Reiner, R. (2010) *The politics of the police* (4th edn), Oxford: Oxford University Press

Questions to consider from this chapter and your further reading

- Should the police change the way they stop and search?
- Will a code of ethics be sufficient in ensuring that the police do not behave in a corrupt manner?
- How might you develop a new culture within the police?

FOUR

The Crown Prosecution Service

Background

In recent years, the Crown Prosecution Service (CPS) has undergone radical shifts in responsibility, many of which have involved the expansion of its role in terms of charging, victim liaison and advocacy. It could be argued that through these changes, the organisation has come to occupy a more prominent role in the processing of criminal cases through the criminal justice system. These changes have represented considerable challenges for the CPS in terms of balancing its central role as the independent reviewer of police decision making, while at the same time working increasingly closely with the police to ensure effective charging and prosecution decision making. Similarly, it must also balance its role as state prosecutors with its increasing responsibility for victims and witnesses, while also ensuring that the public remain confident that it makes its decisions fairly, no matter who is the victim and who is the offender.

It was not until the early part of the 19th century that state intervention in prosecutions became commonplace. Before that, victims brought their own private prosecutions. The police gradually expanded their role in detecting and investigating crime to include initiating prosecutions. In 1879, the role of the Director of Public Prosecutions (DPP) was established to oversee the prosecution of particularly serious or sensitive cases, although the majority of criminal prosecutions continued to be carried out by the police. This arrangement held throughout much of the 20th century, and while most police forces developed a prosecuting solicitors' department to present cases in court, the decision to prosecute remained clearly in the hands of the police.

That changed with the Prosecution of Offenders Act 1985. This Act established the CPS, which began working as an independent prosecuting body the following year. This significant change followed a Royal Commission on Criminal Procedure in 1981, chaired by Sir Cyril Phillips, which recommended that the investigation and prosecution of a crime should not be carried out by the same agency. The Commission argued that the decision to prosecute should be based on an independent and objective assessment of the evidence and should therefore be separate from the process of investigation. Furthermore, it argued that without a separation of duties, the police desire to see a suspect convicted could risk jeopardising due process.

The CPS is therefore a relatively 'new' agency of the criminal justice system and its introduction was not without controversy – most notably with the police service, which lost most of its prosecuting powers. In fact, in its early days, the role of the CPS was very limited – mainly receiving cases that had been investigated and already charged by the police, leading to accusations that the CPS was failing in its remit to stall the momentum of police prosecution even in evidentially weak cases. Subsequently, the CPS saw its powers expand as the Auld Commission in 2001 called for the CPS to take control of cases earlier on in the process:

> The prosecutor should take control of cases at the charge, or where appropriate pre-charge, stage, fix on the right charges from the

start and keep to them ... For all this the Service needs greater legal powers, in particular the power to determine the initial charge, and considerably more resources, in particular trained staff and information technology, than it has had in the first fifteen years of its life. (Auld, 2001, p 399)

The Attorney General and the Home Secretary accepted this recommendation and the subsequent changes set the scene for the current configuration of the CPS that is discussed in the remainder of this chapter. The discussion starts with an overview of the organisation of the CPS, before going on to explore key issues about the nature of charging decisions and the role of the CPS in looking after victims, which highlight tensions between the role of the prosecution service and other agents in the criminal process. A final section explores the ways in which prosecutors can exercise their discretion in decision making and the implications of this for notions of justice.

Organisation and delivery

The CPS is an independent agency, led by the DPP, under the superintendence of the Attorney General who, as a government minister, is accountable to Parliament for the work of the CPS. The CPS is divided into 13 geographical areas, covering police force boundaries throughout England and Wales. Each area is led by a Chief Crown Prosecutor and is responsible for dealing with a wide range of cases across the magistrates' courts and the Crown Court. The CPS also provides a 24/7 service – 'CPS Direct' – which covers all jurisdictions to support the police out of hours. In addition, the CPS operates central Casework Divisions that handle the most complex prosecutions: Specialist Fraud; Special Crime and Counter-terrorism; Organised Crime; International Justice; and the CPS Proceeds of Crime Service.

The CPS is funded by central government via the Attorney General's Office. It also has income-raising powers through 'proceeds of crime' –

the confiscation of assets from serious and organised crime. In 2015-16, this amounted to £84.2 million. The CPS has reduced its expenditure by 20.9% since 2010-11, from £616 million to £487 million in 2015-16. During the same period, the number of people employed by the CPS has fallen by 39%, from 8,300 in 2010-11 to 6,000 in 2016 (see Figure 4.1). A high proportion of CPS employees are women (65% in 2015-16) and 16% of its employees are from BAME groups.

Figure 4.1: CPS staff in post at end of financial year 2010-11 to 2015-16

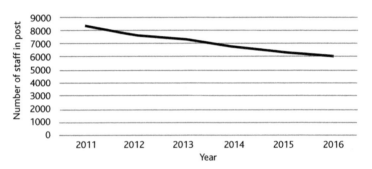

Most CPS lawyers are trained solicitors, although some have a background as a barrister. In addition, the CPS employs around 3,000 caseworkers and administrators. Since the Access to Justice Act 1999, non-legally trained CPS caseworkers, or associate prosecutors, are allowed to present in a limited range of cases in the magistrates' courts. In addition, since 2004, the CPS has gradually moved to a strategy of using in-house advocates, or Crown Advocates, in the Crown Court, rather than relying on external services. The aim of this strategy is to improve consistency in decision making, by allowing the CPS to have greater ownership of a case throughout the criminal justice process. Concerns have been expressed about the quality of some of this advocacy by the CPS Inspectorate, but the introduction of advocacy assessment programmes has sought to improve this.

CPS caseloads (represented by prosecutions) vary, depending on levels of crime, the number of arrests made by the police, the number of cautions and the impact of early involvement of prosecutors. Table 4.1 shows that, overall, caseloads have fallen since 2010-11, from 957,881 to 637,778 in 2015-16 (a reduction of 33%). The proportions of cases in each type of court has also changed, with increasing proportions of prosecutions in the Crown Court (up from 12.2% in 2010-11 to 15.5% in 2015-16). The latter supports the claim by the CPS that although overall caseloads have fallen, there has been an increase in complex cases such as child sexual abuse (up 29% since 2011) and fraud (up 23% since 2011).

Table 4.1: Prosecutions brought by the CPS by court type, 2010-11 to 2015-16

	2010-11	2011-12	2012-13	2013-14	2014-15	2015-16
Crown Court	116,898	107,268	97,182	94,617	100,865	99,062
Magistrates' courts	840,983	787,613	707,777	640,657	563,625	538,716
Total	957,881	894,881	804,959	735,274	664,490	637,778

Source: CPS annual reports and accounts

Function and powers

The CPS undertakes four main functions in the criminal justice process. These are:

- to provide legal advice to the police;
- to decide whether suspects should be charged with a criminal offence and prosecuted;
- to conduct prosecutions in court;

■ to provide information, assistance and support to victims and prosecution witnesses.

The CPS is not responsible for all criminal prosecutions in England and Wales (see Box 4.1), but it does prosecute 75% of cases in the magistrates' courts and 95% in the Crown Court.

Box 4.1: Agencies other than the CPS who undertake criminal prosecutions

Other agencies include:

- ■ local authorities for environmental health prosecutions;
- ■ the Health and Safety Executive;
- ■ the Driver and Vehicle Licensing Agency for non-payment of road tax;
- ■ the RSPCA for offences against animals;
- ■ the Department for Work and Pensions for benefit fraud.

Unlike many other countries' prosecuting bodies, including Procurator Fiscals in Scotland, the CPS has no powers to investigate or to direct a police investigation. It can, however, interview victims and/or witnesses in advance of trial, if the prosecutor considers that such an interview would help to assess the reliability of the witness's evidence and/or assist in understanding complex evidence. These interviews are most likely to take place in serious, indictable-only cases.

The provision of legal advice to the police occurs before a suspect is charged, and includes information about what kinds of evidence might be necessary to go ahead with a charge. The police need this kind of advice quickly – bearing in mind rules about how long they can detain a suspect, for example – so the CPS Direct service provides online access to 24/7 legal advice.

The police require CPS authorisation about the nature of the charge against a suspect in all serious and indictable offence cases. In other, less serious offence categories, the police can decide on the charge. To make their decision about prosecution, the CPS lawyers must refer to the **Code for Crown Prosecutors** (CPS, 2013a) (see Box 4.2) (hereafter 'the Code'). The Code sets out the basic principles that the CPS must consider, when deciding whether to prosecute a case. Failure to do so can lead to judicial review – especially if a decision has been made not to prosecute. Victims also have the right to request a review of CPS decisions not to prosecute (to be discussed later).

The CPS has a two-stage test that a case must satisfy in order to proceed to a prosecution:

- First, the prosecutor reviewing the case must decide whether there is a **realistic prospect of conviction** – through applying **the evidential test**.
- If they decide that there is, then a second test is applied to ascertain whether it is in the **public interest** to prosecute. If there is no realistic prospect of conviction, the case will not be prosecuted, regardless of the public interest.

To pass the **evidential test,** the prosecutor must decide that: 'an objective, impartial and reasonable jury or bench of magistrates' or judge hearing a case alone, and acting in accordance with the law, is more likely than not to convict the defendant of the charged alleged' (Section 4.5 Code for Crown Prosecutors (CPS, 2013a)). To do this, the reviewer must assess the strength, reliability and admissibility of the evidence and any likely defence.

The **public interest test** involves weighing up the various public interest factors in the case for and against prosecution. Key to this is that the decision to prosecute must be a proportionate and appropriate response to the offending behaviour. Public interest factors to be considered include:

- the seriousness of the case;
- the age of the suspect;
- their culpability and level of involvement in the offence;
- the motivation behind the offence (particularly if this involves hostility towards the victim on the grounds of their race, religion, gender, or disability);
- the harm done to the victim and the impact of the offence on them (and their family and/or community);
- any adverse impact there might for the victim in participating in criminal proceedings.

Box 4.2: Selected excerpts from the CPS Full Code Test

The Evidential Stage

> *Para 4.4 Prosecutors must be satisfied that there is sufficient evidence to provide a realistic prospect of conviction against each suspect on each charge. They must consider what the defence case may be, and how it is likely to affect the prospects of conviction. A case which does not pass the evidential stage must not proceed, no matter how serious or sensitive it may be.*

> *Para 4.5 The finding that there is a realistic prospect of conviction is based on the prosecutor's objective assessment of the evidence, including the impact of any defence, and any other information that the suspect has*

put forward or on which he or she might rely. It means that an objective, impartial and reasonable jury or bench of magistrates or judge hearing a case alone, properly directed and acting in accordance with the law, is more likely than not to convict the defendant of the charge alleged. This is a different test from the one that the criminal courts themselves must apply. A court may only convict if it is sure that the defendant is guilty.

Para 4.6 When deciding whether there is sufficient evidence to prosecute, prosecutors should ask themselves the following:

■   *Can the evidence be used in court?*
Prosecutors should consider whether there is any question over the admissibility of certain evidence. In doing so, prosecutors should assess: the likelihood of that evidence being held as inadmissible by the court; and the importance of that evidence in relation to the evidence as a whole.

■   *Is the evidence reliable?*
Prosecutors should consider whether there are any reasons to question the reliability of the evidence, including its accuracy or integrity.

■   *Is the evidence credible?*
Prosecutors should consider whether there are any reasons to doubt the credibility of the evidence.

The Public Interest Stage

Para 4.7 In every case where there is sufficient evidence to justify a prosecution, prosecutors must go on to consider whether a prosecution is required in the public interest.

Para 4.8 It has never been the rule that a prosecution will automatically take place once the evidential stage is met. A prosecution will usually take place unless the prosecutor is satisfied that there are public interest factors tending against prosecution which outweigh those tending in favour. In some cases the prosecutor may be satisfied that the public interest can be properly served by offering the offender the opportunity to have the matter dealt with by an out-of-court disposal rather than bringing a prosecution.

Para 4.12 Prosecutors should consider each of the following questions:

■ *How serious is the offence committed?*
The more serious the offence, the more likely it is that a prosecution is required.

When deciding the level of seriousness of the offence committed, prosecutors should include amongst the factors for consideration the suspect's culpability and the harm to the victim by asking themselves the questions at b) and c).

■ *What is the level of culpability of the suspect?*
Culpability is likely to be determined by the suspect's level of involvement; the extent to which the offending was premeditated and/or planned; whether they have previous criminal convictions and/or out-of-court disposals and any offending whilst on bail; or whilst subject to a court order; whether the offending was or

is likely to be continued, repeated or escalated; and the suspect's age or maturity (see paragraph d) below for suspects under 18).

Prosecutors should also have regard when considering culpability as to whether the suspect is, or was at the time of the offence, suffering from any significant mental or physical ill health as in some circumstances this may mean that it is less likely that a prosecution is required. However, prosecutors will also need to consider how serious the offence was, whether it is likely to be repeated and the need to safeguard the public or those providing care to such persons.

■   *What are the circumstances of and the harm caused to the victim?*
The circumstances of the victim are highly relevant. The greater the vulnerability of the victim, the more likely it is that a prosecution is required. This includes where a position of trust or authority exists between the suspect and victim.

However, the CPS does not act for victims or their families in the same way as solicitors act for their clients, and prosecutors must form an overall view of the public interest.

■   *What is the impact on the community?*
The greater the impact of the offending on the community, the more likely it is that a prosecution is required. In considering this question, prosecutors should have regard to how community is an inclusive term and is not restricted to communities defined by location.

■   *Is prosecution a proportionate response?*
Prosecutors should also consider whether prosecution is proportionate to the likely outcome, and in so doing the following may be relevant to the case under consideration:

The cost to the CPS prosecution service and the wider criminal justice system, especially where it could be regarded as excessive when weighed against any likely penalty

Cases should be capable of being prosecuted in a way that is consistent with principles of effective case management. For example, in a case involving multiple suspects offenders, prosecution might be reserved for the key main participants in order to avoid excessively long and complex proceedings.

■   *Do sources of information require protecting?*
In cases where public interest immunity does not apply, special care should be taken when proceeding with a prosecution where details may need to be made public that could harm sources of information, international relations or national security. It is essential that such cases are kept under continuing review.

Source: CPS, 2013a, pp 12-13

Once a prosecution begins, the CPS continually reviews cases and can overturn decisions to prosecute if, for example, new evidence comes to light. The overall performance of the CPS is most often measured in terms of its 'conviction rate' – that is, the proportion of prosecutions that result in a conviction. The conviction rate gives an indication of the quality of CPS casework – for example in ensuring that the evidential and public interest tests have been appropriately applied. Table 4.2 shows conviction rates for each court since 2010-11 – these have remained fairly consistent at around 83%, although conviction rates in the magistrates' courts are persistently higher than in the Crown Court.

Table 4.2: CPS conviction rates by court type, 2010-11 to 2015-16

	2010-11	2011-12	2012-13	2013-14	2014-15	2015-16
Magistrates' courts	86% (no individual figures available)	86.5%	86.2%	85.7%	84.2%	84.3%
Crown Court		80.8%	80.7%	81.0%	79.4%	79.7%

Source: CPS annual reports and accounts

However, a key responsibility for the CPS is to pursue prosecution in the interests of justice, and not simply to achieve a conviction, which raises some questions about the use of conviction rates as an indicator of CPS performance. Furthermore, criticisms continue to be levied at the CPS with regard to the discretion of officers in the application of both evidential and public interest tests (which are explored in more detail later in this chapter).

While the CPS function is underpinned by principles of consistency and fairness, there are areas where its work seeks to prioritise offences that have come under public scrutiny for failing to provide justice. In particular, the CPS has been at the forefront of debates regarding violence against women. Criticisms of the poor rates of prosecution and convictions in these areas have led to a number of reforms of CPS practice and an annual violence against women crime report gives detailed analysis of rates of prosecution and conviction in key offences.

Table 4.3 summarises the data for three of the main offence types included in the report, and shows that while the number of prosecutions for domestic abuse have risen by almost 20,000, the conviction rate remains under the CPS average of 83% for the period. However, in rape cases the CPS has not managed to increase the number of prosecutions or conviction rates, highlighting the persistent problems that the police and prosecutors face in this area.

Table 4.3: Prosecutions and conviction rates for selected violence against women offences, 2010-11 and 2015-16

	2010-11		2015-16	
	Number of prosecutions	Conviction rate	Number of prosecutions	Conviction rate
Domestic abuse	82,187	71.9%	100,930	74.5%
Rape	4,208	58.6%	4,643	57.9%
Forced marriage	41	48.8%	53	60.4%

Source: CPS, 2016

Key debates

This section focuses on two issues that represent ongoing debates about the relationship between the CPS and two key agents of the criminal justice system – the police and victims/witnesses. First, regarding the police, the discussion surrounding discontinuance and the Statutory Charging Scheme highlights ongoing debates about 'who' should charge and for what seriousness of offence. Appropriate charging decisions are crucial for the operation of efficient justice systems – no one wants lots of cases to be dropped or trials to be broken with the ensuing impact on victims and the costs involved.

Second, the discussion turns to the expectations placed on the CPS to support victims, which raises questions about what their role should be in this regard where due process might argue that the CPS should be impartial in its prosecuting function and not focused on victim satisfaction.

Discontinuance and the Statutory Charging Scheme

Until the Criminal Justice Act 2003, the police made the initial decision to charge a suspect, albeit they may well discuss the charge with the CPS first – particularly in more complex cases. However, in 2001 the Auld Commission identified an issue with a police tendency to overcharge and a CPS failure to rectify this at review. At the recommendation of Auld, the 2003 Act brought in the **Statutory Charging Scheme (SCS)**, which required that the CPS take the charging decisions in all indictable-only and 'triable either way' offences, leaving the lesser charging decisions (usually involving summary offences) to the police. The idea behind this system is that all charging decisions are subjected to the full evidential and public interest tests at the earliest possible stage. This should result in the weeding out of weak cases and thus a narrowing of the justice gap – that is the attrition rate between recorded offences and subsequent convictions. It was also thought that this system would result in a reduction in any delay in deciding on the correct charge; a reduction in overcharging; a reduction in the number of discontinued cases and 'cracked' trials;[1] more early guilty pleas; and a reduction in the overall time from charge to disposal (Brownlee, 2004).

Since 2003, some charging decisions have been returned to the police, as it was recognised that involving the CPS in more minor cases was resulting in an unnecessarily overly bureaucratic process. Current charging practice allows the police to decide a significant proportion of charging decisions (see Box 4.3), accounting for around 70% of decisions in 2013-14. There remain concerns, however, that the police sometimes charge in cases where the CPS should do so, and conversely that they send cases to the CPS when they could have made this decision themselves.

Box 4.3: Police charging responsibilities

Police may charge:

Any Summary Only offence irrespective of plea;

Any offence of retail theft (shoplifting) or attempted retail theft irrespective of plea provided it is suitable for sentence in the magistrates' courts;

Any either-way offence anticipated as a guilty plea and suitable for sentence in the magistrates' courts;

Provided that this is not:

A case requiring the consent to prosecute of the DPP or law officer;

A case involving a death;

Connected with terrorist activity or official secrets;

Classified as Hate Crime or Domestic Violence under CPS Policies;

An offence of Violent Disorder or Affray;

Causing Grievous Bodily Harm or Wounding, or Actual Bodily Harm;

A Sexual Offences Act offence committed by or upon a person under 18;

An offence under the Licensing Act 2003.

Source: CPS, 2013b

The majority of charging decisions are made through the CPS Direct service (around 85%) rather than through face-to-face meetings with investigators. In the period leading up to court proceedings, the prosecutor will regularly review a case and decide whether it is still appropriate to proceed to prosecution or whether a case should be discontinued. The CPS can decide to discontinue at any stage up to the point when a guilty plea has been entered or a trial has started at magistrates' courts – or prior to the indictment being laid at the Crown Court. However, since its beginning, the CPS has been criticised for discontinuing too many cases – possibly because prior to the SCS the police charged without consultation with the CPS and the CPS discontinued on review. Thus, by bringing the CPS into the charging decision through the SCS, it is argued that the original charge should be more accurate and therefore the need to discontinue less frequent. Table 4.4 shows that the discontinuance rate has dropped from 15.5% in 2002-03 (when the SCS was introduced) to 10.5% in 2014-15.

The CPS Inspectorate reviewed the reasons behind discontinuance in 2007 (HMCPSI, 2007) and found that the reasons behind discontinuance were as follows: insufficient evidence (42.7%); not in the public interest (23.7%); and unable to proceed (25.9%). Examples of the latter include cases where the police file has not been received; the CPS is not ready; the victim or witness refuses to give evidence or retracts; or the victim or witness fails to attend court unexpectedly. The Inspectorate found that domestic violence cases were particularly susceptible to discontinuance, with 24.4% of such cases being discontinued in 2005-06. They suggest in these cases that while there might be sufficient evidence to move to prosecution, over time victims can withdraw their support for that prosecution, often because of the complex nature of their relationship to the defendant.

Table 4.4: CPS annual discontinuance rates, 2002-15

Year	Discontinuance rate (%)
2002-03	15.5
2003-04	13.8
2004-05	12.5
2005-06	11.8
2006-07	10.9
2007-08	9.9
2008-09	8.7
2009-10	9.0
2010-11	9.6
2011-12	9.6
2012-13	9.6
2013-14	9.7
2014-15	10.5

Source: CPS annual reports and accounts, 2003-04 to 2014-15

Supporting victims and witnesses

The Government White Paper *Justice for all* (Ministry of Justice, 2002) called for a rebalancing of the criminal justice system in favour of victims and witnesses. Since then, the CPS, along with other criminal justice agencies, has come under considerable pressure to improve the service it provides to victims and witnesses. This shift presents a significant challenge for the CPS, given a central premise of the criminal justice system is that the prosecutor works on behalf of the state and not on behalf of individual victims of crime. The House of Commons Justice Committee drew attention to this dilemma in 2009. It expressed considerable concern that while policy and practice developments aimed at improving the service offered to victims should be welcomed, presenting the CPS as some kind of champion for the victim was 'a damaging misrepresentation of reality' (House of Commons Justice Committee, 2009), which would only serve to raise unrealistic expectations in victims. The committee was also adamant that the proper separation of prosecutors and victims must be maintained, if the criminal justice system was to remain fair and impartial for defendants.

These concerns notwithstanding there is no doubt that the CPS, evident in numerous policy documents and guidance, now emphasises its role in supporting victims and witnesses through the criminal justice process and uses language in these documents that echoes the *Justice for All* rhetoric to place victims at the heart of the criminal justice system. The latest version of the Prosecutors' Pledge is a clear example (see Box 4.4).

Box 4.4: The Prosecutors' Pledge

'Take into account the impact on the victim or their family when making a Charging decision ...'

'Inform the victim where the charge is withdrawn, discontinued or substantially altered ...'

'When practical seek a victim's view or that of the family when considering the acceptability of a plea ...'

'Address the specific needs of a victim and where justified seek to protect their identity by making an appropriate application to the court ...'

'Assist victims at court to refresh their memory from their written or video statement and answer their questions on court procedure and processes ...'

'Promote and encourage two-way communication between victim and prosecutor at court ...'

'Protect victims from unwarranted or irrelevant attacks on their character and may seek the court's intervention where cross-examination is considered to be inappropriate or oppressive ...'

'On conviction, robustly challenge defence mitigation which is derogatory to a victim's character ...'

'On conviction, apply for appropriate order for compensation, restitution or future protection of the victim ...'

'Keep victims informed of the progress of any appeal, and explain the effect of the court's judgment ...'

Source: For full details, go to: www.cps.gov.uk/publications/prosecution/prosecutor_pledge.html

---

The CPS has the central responsibility within the modern criminal justice system in keeping victims and witnesses informed, particularly in cases involving a trial. Many of these CPS responsibilities stem from the revised the Code of Practice for Victims of Crime (MOJ, 2015a), which outlines the responsibilities for all criminal justice agencies towards victims. In addition, obligations under the Human Rights Act 1998 require public authorities to act in ways that are compatible with the human rights of victims and witnesses.

As a result of this new responsibility, the CPS has now developed dedicated victim liaison units in each area. These dedicated units are responsible for: informing victims of CPS decisions to stop proceedings or substantially alter a charge; the administration of the Victims' Right to Review (VRR) and the Victim Communication and Liaison schemes; and the management of complaints and feedback received.

Under the Victim Communication and Liaison scheme, the CPS must communicate to victims a decision not to prosecute, to discontinue, to withdraw or to substantially alter a charge and the reasons for doing so. In more serious cases, such as those involving a death, and sexual or hate crimes, a meeting must be offered to the victim to discuss those decisions.

In June 2013, the CPS launched the VRR scheme following the Court of Appeal decision in *R v Christopher Killick*,[2] in which the Court concluded that victims should have a right to seek a review of a CPS decision not to prosecute and should not have to seek recourse to judicial review in order to do so. Box 4.5 outlines when a victim can request a review of the decision not to prosecute. It is important to note that this only applies to cases where that decision was made after 5 June 2013.

Box 4.5: *Victim's Right to Review guidance* (DPP, 2016)

The right to review arises where the CPS:

- makes the decision not to bring proceedings (at the pre-charge stage);
- decides to discontinue (or withdraw in the magistrates' courts) **all** charges involving the victim, thereby entirely ending **all** proceedings relating to them;
- offers no evidence in **all** proceedings relating to the victim; or
- decides to leave **all** charges in the proceedings to lie on file.

It is clear from this that not all cases will offer such an opportunity – particularly those where *some* charges against *some* suspects relating to the victim are going ahead. Nevertheless, the CPS must now write to a victim to explain its decision not to prosecute and in that letter it must inform the victim that they have the right to seek a review and how to do so. The review will initially take place in the local CPS office by a different prosecutor. If the victim is still unhappy about the decision made in that review, they can then ask that the case be considered by the Appeals and Reviews Unit at CPS Headquarters or by the area's Chief Crown Prosecutor. Between 1 April 2014 and 31 March 2015, the CPS reviewed 1,674 cases and decisions in 1,464 of those cases were found to be the right one. In total, 210 decisions have been overturned, which accounts for 0.17% of all qualifying decisions finalised in the period.

Focus on prosecutorial discretion

Crown Prosecutors are able to exercise considerable discretion when deciding whether or not to proceed with a prosecution – albeit that that decision must be based on the Code as explained earlier. While the CPS would argue that its Code is publicly available and that therefore its decision-making process is completely transparent, since its inception, the CPS has come under considerable and sustained criticism that it is too close to the police and therefore too 'prosecution-minded'. That is, instead of being entirely objective when assessing the realistic prospect of conviction or the public interest criteria, it inevitably veers towards proceeding to a prosecution. While CPS decisions can be challenged, the courts 'have expressed reluctance to interfere with prosecutorial discretion, emphasising that their power to review decisions is to be exercised sparingly' (Burton, 2001, p 374).

Discretion on the grounds of evidence

The CPS has been accused of being particularly reluctant to prosecute in cases where the defendant is a police officer or a prison officer – most notably in cases involving deaths in custody. Gerald Butler QC observed in his 1999 review of CPS decision making in cases of deaths in custody (Butler, 1999) that there is a common perception within the criminal justice system that juries tend to be reluctant to convict in cases where the defendant is a police or prison officer. He suggested that this might result in a prosecutor applying a more stringent approach to the **evidential test**. While this might be understandable, it goes against the essence of the Code, which clearly states that all subjective elements must be put aside and that the prosecutor must not take into account their own opinions of the propensity of juries to convict in such cases. That is, they should resist predicting outcomes in specific cases and look solely at the evidence as it stands. Similarly, Butler (1999) highlights certain parts of the Code, which he feels are the essence of its intent to be fair:

> Crown Prosecutors must be fair, independent and objective. They must not let their personal views of the ethnic or national origin, sex, religious beliefs, political views or sexual preference of the offender, victim or witness influence their decisions. They must also not be affected by improper or undue pressure from any source. Prosecutors must always act in the interests of justice and not solely for the purpose of obtaining a conviction. (Section 2.4, The Code for Crown Prosecutors)

> The Crown Prosecution Service and the police work closely together to reach the right decision, but the final responsibility for the decision rests with the Crown Prosecution Service (Section 3.6, The Code for Crown Prosecutors). (Quoted in Butler, 1999)

Butler QC recommended that reasons should be given in cases where the coroner's inquest has recorded a verdict of unlawful killing but a decision has been made not to prosecute. He found that in the two cases he reviewed – *O'Brien* and *Lapite*[3] – the CPS review about whether to prosecute had involved misunderstandings and misapplications of the law. The lack of available routes whereby victims can challenge CPS decisions has resulted in developments to allow more scope for victims and victims' families to question CPS decision making short of judicial review, such as the VRR as highlighted in the previous section.

However, only families whose relatives died in custody since June 2013 will be able to use the VRR.

Box 4.6 outlines the CPS review of the unlawful killing of Alton Manning, who died in prison custody.

Box 4.6: *R v DPP Ex p. Manning* Q.B. 330 (QBD (Admin))

Alton Manning died in December 1995 after being asphyxiated during a struggle with prison officers when they carried him away from his cell. Mr Manning had been asked to strip and squat down so that he could also be searched in the genital and anal area for drugs. According to prison officers, Mr Manning attempted to assault one of them, and he was carried forcibly in a restraint position out of the cell. Other prisoners who witnessed the events testified at the coroner's inquest that the headlock employed during that restraint by one prison officer was dangerous. By the time the officers had carried Mr Manning to the dining area he was not breathing and all attempts to revive him failed. He was found to be bleeding from the ear and nose – which is associated with undue pressure being placed on the neck.

Following the verdict of unlawful killing at the inquest, the CPS reviewed their initial decision that there had not been a **realistic prospect of conviction** in this case, but the review came to the same conclusion. The sisters of Mr Manning went to the High Court to ask for a judicial review of the CPS decision. The High Court quashed the decision not to prosecute; criticised the fact that the CPS was not obliged to give a reason to Mr Manning's family for their decision; and concluded that the prosecutor had applied **a higher standard** than the realistic prospect of conviction set out in the Code which suggested that their discretion was not applied in a legitimate or fair way.

Source: Burton, 2001

Discretion on the grounds of public interest

It could be argued that it is the public interest test that is most directly linked with CPS discretion, because this allows prosecutors to decide *against* prosecution, even when there is sufficient evidence to proceed to charge and court. However, in order for there to be public confidence that the assessment is made fairly and consistently we, as a society, need to understand what criteria are taken into account and be confident that prosecutors are using their discretion appropriately, consistently and without discrimination.

The importance of public confidence in CPS application of the public interest assessment is clearly illustrated by cases involving assisted suicide. The offence of encouraging or assisting a suicide is very serious, carrying a maximum penalty of 14 years' imprisonment. Given this, the assessment would generally be in favour of prosecution, on the basis of that seriousness. However, in recent years, several cases of English citizens travelling to Switzerland[4] to commit suicide have raised concerns that the criteria were not sufficiently clear in terms of whether family members who assisted their loved ones would be subject to prosecution on their return to England.

Debbie Purdy who suffered from progressive multiple sclerosis sought a ruling from the House of Lords to help establish whether her husband would face prosecution, if he helped her travel to Switzerland to commit suicide.[5] She asked that the DPP set out the factors that would be taken into consideration when deciding if someone would face prosecution for helping someone else to die. The House of Lords asked the DPP to clarify his position on assisted suicide and he consequently issued guidance in 2010[6] outlining in detail what criteria, particularly in terms of public interest, would be taken into account. The key factors in the guidance centre on whether:the victim had reached a 'voluntary, clear, settled and informed' decision (para 45.1); the suspect was 'wholly motivated by compassion' (para 45.3); the suspect had sought to dissuade the victim; (para 45.4); the suspect had only been involved in minor and/ or reluctant assistance in 'the face of a determined wish on the part of the victim' (paras 45.4–45.5).

While Debbie Purdy was not able to fulfil her wish to travel to Switzerland as she became too ill, several others have taken that journey, and their friends and relatives have not faced charges based on the 2010 guidance. In fact, there has only been one conviction of assisted (attempted) suicide since the guidance was published. Box 4.7 outlines the public interest decision-making test in a typical assisted suicide case involving travelling to Switzerland.

Box 4.7: The death of Raymond Cutkelvin

Mr Cutkelvin was diagnosed with pancreatic cancer in 2006, for which he declined treatment. He contacted Dignitas, a Swiss assisted suicide charity, in October 2006 and was given consent by them to access an assisted suicide after he joined the charity in January 2007. He travelled to Switzerland in February 2007 with his civil partner, Alan Rees, and Dr Michael Urwin, a close friend and relative. He drank a lethal dose of medication and thereby ended his life.

A police investigation into the case only started when a newspaper article appeared some two years later and the actions of Mr Rees and Dr Urwin were investigated. In reaching his decision not to charge either of the men, the then DPP, Keir Starmer, stated that while there was sufficient evidence to prosecute both, such a prosecution would not be in the public interest according to the CPS policy:

> By applying the Policy for Prosecutors in respect of cases of encouraging or assisting suicide, I have concluded that none of the public interest factors in favour of prosecution apply in Mr Rees' cases. The evidence shows that Mr Cutkelvin was a strong-minded man who had the capacity to reach an informed decision to commit suicide and he clearly did so without any pressure from Mr Rees or anyone else. Mr Rees acted throughout as a supportive and loving partner and was wholly motivated by compassion … I have [also] concluded that Mr Cutkelvin had a clear intention to commit suicide and would have done so without any assistance from Dr Irwin. Dr Irwin was not out to gain for himself and has fully cooperated with police enquiries. He is now 79 years old and although there is evidence that he received a caution in 2004 for an offence related to assisted suicide, it is highly unlikely … that the court would impose anything other than a nominal penalty on him. (Keir Starmer, DPP, 25 June 2010)

Summary

- The CPS is a relatively new agency of the criminal justice system, established in 1985 to separate the process of investigation (undertaken by the police) from the decision to prosecute.
- Thirteen CPS areas are responsible for the majority of prosecutions across 43 police force areas. A 24/7 CPS Direct service provides out-of-hours support for charging decisions.
- CPS prosecutions must satisfy an 'evidential test' and a 'public interest' test, to ensure that there is both a realistic prospect of conviction and that it is in the public interest to do so.
- Statutory charging systems have been in place since 2003 to reduce mistakes in charging decisions and to ensure that trials are not discontinued.
- The role of the CPS has expanded to include victim liaison and advocacy, raising questions about its role as independent prosecutor for the state, while keeping victims and witnesses engaged and satisfied with their treatment.

Guide to data sources and other online resources

Data used in this chapter is derived from the following sources

- *CPS annual reports and accounts* – these contain information about key performance measures, including conviction rates, number of prosecutions, changes in workforce and expenditure: http://cps.gov.uk/data/annual_report/index.html
- *CPS equality and diversity workforce* reports provide further details about the workforce: http://cps.gov.uk/data/equality_and_diversity/index.html
- *Violence against women and girls* crime reports give in-depth analysis of prosecution and conviction across a range of specific crimes: www.cps.gov.uk/publications/docs/cps_vawg_report_2016.pdf

Other websites of interest

- ▣ HM Crown Prosecution Service Inspectorate: https://www.justiceinspectorates.gov.uk/hmcpsi
- ▣ CPS guidance on working with victims and witnesses: http://www.cps.gov.uk/victims_witnesses/

Taking it further ...

More in-depth reading about the issues raised in this chapter

Brownlee, I.D. (2004) The statutory charging scheme in England and Wales: Towards a unified prosecution system?, *Criminal Law Review*, 896-907Burton, M. (2001) Reviewing Crown Prosecution Service decisions not to prosecute, *Criminal Law Review*, 374-84

Daw, R. and Solomon, A. (2010) Assisted suicide and identifying the public interest in the decision to prosecute, *Criminal Law Review*, 737-51

Hall, M. (2010) The relationship between victims and prosecutors: Defending victims' rights?, *Criminal Law Review*, 1, 31-45

Questions to consider from this chapter and your further reading

- ■ Would more distance between the police and the CPS make for fairer decision-making processes?
- ■ Should there be a separate prosecution body for cases involving criminal justice agents as defendants?
- ■ Should prosecutors act on behalf of victims or the state?

Notes

1   A 'cracked trial' is one that is listed as a not guilty plea, but where at a very late stage the defendant changes his or her mind and pleads guilty.

2   *R v Christopher Killick* [2011] EWCA Crim 1608 (*R v Killick*).

3   Richard O'Brien was arrested in 1994 on suspicion of being drunk and disorderly. He lost consciousness whilst in police custody and was pronounced dead on arrival at Hospital. In the same year, Shiji Lapite was arrested after he left a club in east London on suspicion of carrying crack cocaine. During a struggle, one officer applied a neckhold and the other kicked Mr Lapite in the head. Half an hour later he was dead from suspected asphyxiation.

4   Assisted suicide is legal in Switzerland.

5   *R (on the application of Purdy) v DPP* [2009] UKHL 45.

6   Updated in October 2014. See: www.cps.gov.uk/publications/prosecution/assisted_suicide_policy.html

FIVE

The criminal courts

Background

The courtroom is the ultimate stage in a suspect's journey to either punishment or acquittal – all the preceding elements of the justice system are put to the test here. Have the police investigated the crime with due respect to the law and collected evidence that is sufficient to secure a conviction? Will the prosecution be able to persuade the jury, beyond reasonable doubt, that the suspect is guilty? Will victims achieve the justice they crave? Given the enormity of the decisions that might be made, and the repercussions for everyone involved, it is no surprise that the courtroom, with presiding judge and rituals dating back hundreds of years, provides a powerful representation of the idea of justice.

In fact, our modern court system stems from the time of Henry II (1154-89). In 1166, Henry issued a Declaration at the Assize of Clarendon, which began the process of judges travelling the country – which was divided into different circuits – deciding cases. This came to be known as the Assizes System, which survived until 1971. Laws were made by the judges in Westminster, meaning that national laws applied to everyone and so were common to all – thus 'common law'.

Over time, a second type of court began to evolve – that we now call the magistrates' court. Justices of the Peace or magistrates were commissioned to oversee these courts, and it is they who have undertaken the majority of the judicial work carried out in England and Wales since that time. The Judiciary website tells us that Crown Courts were established in 1956. The Royal Commission on Assizes and Quarter Sessions, 1966-69, led to the abolition of courts of assize and quarter sessions and the establishment of a new Crown Court to deal with business from both, under the terms of the Courts Act 1971.

The court is often described as a place of 'resolution' – where disputes are settled; but it is important not to confuse 'resolution' with 'truth', because the nature of the legal system in England and Wales is not predicated on the assumption of truth-finding, but rather on proving the suspect guilty. This 'adversarial system' requires the prosecution to establish its case for a guilty verdict. It is then up to the defence to undermine the prosecution case, by introducing 'reasonable doubt'. This competitive process is very different to the inquisitorial system that operates throughout most European countries (see Box 5.1) and is much criticised for the impact it might have on victims and witnesses, who are subjected to intense cross-examination as each side battles to undermine each other's arguments.

With its rituals and costumes, arguments and legalese, the courtroom can be an alien environment for anyone seeking justice, although in reality only a small proportion of cases come to be heard in the classic courtroom represented by judge, jury and counsel. Despite this, the operation of justice in public view, with attendant civic involvement in the form of a lay jury, remains at the heart of our understanding of justice.

The aim of this chapter is to describe how the court system in England and Wales is organised and the different functions and powers ascribed to different courts. In rehearsing key debates, the discussion focuses on

1166 Declaration at the Assize of Clarendon ⟳ **1967** Criminal Justice Act ⟳

key aspects of 'justice': the issues surrounding the use of a lay jury in decision making; the ways in which miscarriages of justice can occur; and how those who believe they have been wrongly convicted can appeal. Each of these debates raises important questions about the capacity of the court system to ensure justice for all.

A final section explores the issue of diversity within the judiciary and legal profession – as key stakeholders in the pursuit of justice, it is of interest to consider the extent to which some of the most powerful people working in the justice system can be seen to represent the society they serve.

Box 5.1: Inquisitorial system

In an inquisitorial system, the key scrutiny of the evidence is done by the court – in some systems a judge; in others a magistrate. In this system, it is the judge or magistrate (known as the *juge d'instruction*)[1] who receives a dossier of evidence gathered by the police and prosecution. The judge then decides who to call as witnesses, and questions those witnesses him or herself. It is argued that this process is more focused on an objective search for truth, since there are no opposing parties who may be tempted to suppress or ignore evidence that does not support their version of events. Risks can occur, however, since in the construction of that dossier, investigators may have a particular view of the case and may exclude evidence that might undermine that view. The contents of the dossier may also influence the magistrate or judge, which risks partiality towards the prosecution case, rather than the judge acting as an independent arbiter of the evidence.

1971 Courts Act 🟡 **1972** Criminal Justice Act 🟡 **1974** Juries Act 🟡 **1980** Magistrates Court Act

Organisation and delivery

The court process in England in Wales is organised around a two-tier system based on seriousness of offence (see the 'Function and powers' section later in this chapter). There are currently around 330 magistrates' courts operating throughout England and Wales, but there have been significant closures since austerity measures were implemented in 2010, resulting in the loss of 93 magistrates' courts and 49 county courts.

The magistrates' court is presided over by either a sole district judge (legally qualified) or a panel of three 'lay' magistrates. The lay magistracy are not legally qualified and, apart from expenses, are unpaid volunteers. Because magistrates are lay workers, they require advice about the law. This is provided by their justices' clerk or legal adviser in the court, all of whom are qualified barristers or solicitors.

The idea of the magistrates' courts is to offer swift, summary justice:

> a prompt and relatively inexpensive response to crime: the meting out of early sanctions and the provision of hopefully swift remedies ... for comparatively minor offending behaviour ... its principle function ... is to provide the forum in which all criminal prosecutions are initiated and most decided. (Ministry of Justice, 2002)

Magistrates' courts have a number of advantages other than the provision of swift justice, which has meant that increasing the number of cases processed in them has received considerable governmental support. For example, the limited sentencing powers of magistrates mean that fewer people are sentenced to custody and the cost of processing cases is far less than in the Crown Court. There have been various suggestions put forward therefore to limit the types of cases that go to the Crown Court, such as removing the right of defendants to elect for Crown Court in 'triable either way' offences. However,

1994 Police and Magistrates Court Act ⮑ **1997** Criminal Cases Review Commission begins operating ⮑

these have not yet translated into legislation – perhaps reflecting the centrality of our right to be tried before a jury of our peers (to be discussed later).

Unlike the magistrates' courts, the Crown Court is a single entity – sitting in 77 court centres across England and Wales. There are three different types of Crown Court centre, based on the type of work they deal with, and hence the seniority of the judiciary who visit them:

- **First-tier centres** – visited by High Court judges for Crown Court criminal and High Court civil work. Around a quarter of the total number of centres are designated first tier. They are mostly located in areas with high populations (Bristol, Birmingham, Manchester, for example), or central towns serving a large area (Norwich, Truro, Carlisle, for example).
- **Second-tier centres** – visited by High Court judges for Crown Court criminal work only. Around a quarter of Crown Court centres are designated second tier.
- **Third-tier centres** – not normally visited by High Court judges handling Crown Court criminal work only. Third-tier centres make up around half of all centres.

Circuit judges and recorders deal with Crown Court criminal work in all three types of centre.

The court system is funded by central government via the Ministry of Justice and Her Majesty's Courts and Tribunals Service (HMCTS). Its accounts show that since 2010-11, expenditure has fallen by 25% from £1.569 billion to £1.178 billion. These reductions are not equally dispersed throughout the agency, however: judicial staff costs have risen through the same period from £4.5 million in 2010-11 to £4.6 million in 2015-16, while non-judicial staff costs have fallen from £6.2 million to £5.0 million for the same period.

1999 Youth Justice and Criminal Evidence Act ⟳ **1999** Launch of the Equal Treatment Bench Book ⟳

Excluding the judiciary, HMCTS employs around 16,000 people. Staff numbers have fallen in HMCTS by 27.5% in the period – representing 4,491 posts. Figure 5.1 shows the overall trends since 2010-11. Workforce data shows that 70% of the HMCTS workforce is female and of those who declared, 65% were white and 14% black and minority ethnic (BAME). Concerns have long been expressed that the judiciary falls short of representing the increasingly diverse society it serves. Issues of judicial diversity are considered in more detail in the 'Focus on ...' section at the end of this chapter.

Figure 5.1: HMCTS staff, 2010-11 to 2015-16

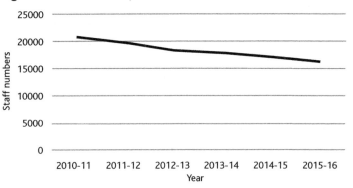

In 2016, there were 17,552 magistrates and 3,202 judges presiding over courts in England and Wales. In 2010-11, the figures were 26,237 and 3,373 respectively. The falling numbers of magistrates reflect overall reductions in workloads and the increasing use of out-of-court disposals. Aside from the judiciary, much court work does not require legal training – most of the work involves administrative and security duties, such as ushers and clerks.

In terms of workloads, the courts depend on those decisions made by the police (arrest) and CPS (charge and prosecution) as well as the amount and types of crime that are committed. Table 5.1 shows that the number of trials held in each court since 2010 has fallen by 10%, with 201,703 trials taking place in 2015. The proportion of trials held across each type of court remains fairly stable, with magistrates' courts responsible for around 80% of all trials in the period.

Table 5.1: Number of trials by type of court, January 2010 to December 2015

Court	2010	2011	2012	2013	2014	2015	% change
Magistrates' court	179,794	166,808	156,671	155,087	158,984	162,668	-10.5
Crown Court	43,259	41,703	38,432	33,669	35,974	39,035	-10.8
Total	223,053	208,511	195,103	188,756	194,958	201,703	
Proportion of Crown Court	19.4	20.0	19.7	17.8	18.5	19.4	

Source: HMCTS annual reports and accounts

The costs of different kinds of trials is almost impossible to estimate, although the additional time taken to complete Crown Court trials along with additional judicial costs and jury costs make these significantly more costly overall than those in magistrates' courts.

Function and powers

The criminal courts, as perhaps the name suggests, deal with criminal law as defined by the state. They have the power to decide what behaviour is subject to punishment and what instead might more appropriately be dealt with through civil or private cases. As such, the criminal court is dealing with offences against the public realm and not individual victims (hence the standard use of *R v Offender* where 'R' indicates Regina and not the name of the victim). Thus, it is the power of the state versus a defendant that is tried in court – hence the need

2003 Courts Act 🔵 **2003** Criminal Justice Act 🔵

for rules and procedures to protect defendants that are often seen to be more rigorous than in civil (non-criminal) proceedings. The most common way of articulating these tighter procedures is with regard to the extent to which a case needs to be proven: in the criminal court it is 'beyond reasonable doubt', whereas in civil proceedings it is 'on the balance of probabilities'. Consequently, the court system makes much of its role in the pursuit of justice, which is neatly summarised in the description that HMCTS gives of its core function:

> Our role is to to run an efficient and effective courts and tribunals system to support the delivery of justice. We enable the rule of law to be upheld through our administration, we provide access to justice, and we provide the support to enable the judiciary, tribunal members and the magistracy to exercise their judicial functions independently. (HMCTS, 2016)

In doing so, it has responsibility for the running of both types of court, although each of these plays a different role in the administration of justice, and they have different sentencing powers.

Magistrates deal with two kinds of cases:

- **Summary offences** – these are less serious cases, such as motoring offences and minor assaults, where the defendant is not usually entitled to trial by jury. They are generally disposed of in magistrates' courts.
- **'Triable either way' offences** – these cases can be dealt with either by magistrates or before a judge and jury at the Crown Court. All defendants have the right to elect for trial at the Crown Court. Alternatively, magistrates might decide that a case is sufficiently serious that it should be dealt with in the Crown Court – because the sentence that can be imposed at the magistrates' court will be inadequate.

2004 Appointment of the first female Law Lord (Brenda Hale) **2005** Constitutional Reform Act

If the case is to be dealt with at a magistrates' court, the defendant is asked to enter a plea. If they plead guilty or are later found to be guilty, the magistrates can impose a sentence, generally of up to six months' imprisonment for a single offence (12 months in total), or a fine, generally of up to £5,000. They can also use the full range of community sentences available to them. There are sentencing guidelines to which magistrates must refer – but these are only guidelines. Like the police, the CPS and judges, magistrates use their own judgement and discretion in deciding upon a sentence. Even in indictable-only cases, the magistrates' court will initially decide whether to grant bail and consider other legal issues, such as reporting restrictions, before passing the case on to the Crown Court.

The Crown Court deals with serious criminal cases, which include:

- cases sent for trial by magistrates' courts because the offences are 'indictable only';
- 'triable either way' offences (which can be heard in a magistrate's court, but can also be sent to the Crown Court if the defendant chooses a jury trial);
- defendants convicted in magistrates' courts, but sent to the Crown Court for sentencing due to the seriousness of the offence;
- appeals against decisions of magistrates' courts.

At the Crown Court, the judge decides on matters of law, such as admissibility of evidence, and ensures that the trial is run fairly and properly. The jury decides on matters of fact in order to decide whether the defendant is guilty of the charges laid. Any questions of law will be dealt with by the judge in the absence of the jury, so that the case will not be prejudiced by any matters raised. It is only once the judge has decided that a piece of evidence is admissible that the jury will hear of it.

If there is to be a trial before judge and jury at the Crown Court, the purpose of that trial is to determine whether the accused person is guilty on the basis of the evidence put before the court by the prosecution and the countervailing arguments of the defence. It is essential to remember, however, that the vast majority of cases do not entail a trial, because most defendants plead guilty. For example, of the 87,212 offenders sentenced in the Crown Court in 2015-16, a total of 77,130 (90%) pleaded guilty and 10,082 were found guilty after a trial.

There are likely to be many factors that influence the decision whether and when to plead guilty. At the charging stage, the prosecution may wish to secure a guilty plea to a lesser charge, because they believe they will find it difficult to prove the more serious offence in court. For the accused, this is beneficial, as the sentencing options are likely to be less severe for that less serious offence. For the prosecution, it makes their lives far less complicated in terms of not having to prepare a full case for the prosecution on the more serious charge, while still securing a conviction and sentence for some form of offence.

Offenders are likely to plead guilty at an early stage, if they believe that by doing so they will avoid a custodial sentence – particularly if they plead guilty to a lesser charge. Statistics from the Sentencing Council show some evidence of this in the Crown Court; a lower proportion of offenders who pleaded guilty were sentenced to immediate custody (53%) compared to those that pleaded not guilty (71%). Even if defendants do not avoid custody, they will still receive a discount on a custodial sentence (up to one third for a guilty plea entered at the earliest possible opportunity). The courts also benefit when a defendant pleads guilty at this stage, because they save a great deal of court time. Cases will also come to court more quickly, avoiding delays in procedures that can be particularly difficult for victims. In addition, victims and witnesses are spared having to appear at court to testify, and the police and the CPS can free up their resources for the investigation and prosecution of other cases. However, the emphasis

2014 Legal Aid, Sentencing and Punishment of Offenders Act

on increasing guilty plea rates also risks serious cases being dealt with too leniently, or alternatively may cause innocent people to plead guilty for fear of not being believed at trial and incurring a heavier sentence. It also removes the public scrutiny of evidence, given that no evidence is presented in open court. This means that important aspects of due process protections do not come into play.

It is the judge's role to regulate the proceedings in the Crown Court; they will determine the admissibility of the evidence and ensure that the trial is conducted fairly and all practices and procedures are strictly adhered to. At the end of a trial, the judge sums up the case for the jury and guides them through the evidence. If the defendant is convicted, the judge then passes sentence. In order to do this, the judge will listen to mitigating factors presented by the defence and aggravating factors presented by the prosecution. For offences that might result in a custodial sentence, the judge will also ask for a pre-sentence report to be completed by the National Probation Service (see Chapter Seven).

Thus, there are key differences in the way that these tiers of justice operate, and consequently differences in the cost of running them and the outcomes for offenders.

Key debates

There are fundamental issues underpinning concepts of justice that are most obviously represented in the courtroom, which provide the context to the key issues that are discussed in this section. The first relates to the use of trial by jury as a mechanism for the law to be held accountable to the wishes of the people, although this is not without difficulties, as we shall see. One of the problems that a jury faces is complex evidence, and our focus on miscarriages of justice highlights the problematic role of expert witness evidence in trial proceedings. Finally, justice demands that those who have been wrongly convicted have the right to appeal, so this section ends with a description of appeals processes.

Trial by jury

The principle of our right to be tried before a jury of our peers is central to our criminal justice system, though it is worth repeating that a jury will be called only in the minority of indictable-only offences where the defendant enters a not guilty plea. The jury represents the idea that public opinion about the law, about fairness and about justice can be fed into the criminal justice system through their civic participation. Thus, unfair laws or oppressive actions by the state can be called into question by, for example, a jury finding a technically guilty defendant innocent because they do not believe a conviction represents justice in the particular circumstances of the case.

The jury comprises 12 individuals between 18 and 70 years of age, who are drawn at random from the electoral register. The aim is to ensure a cross-representation of society on juries, although some people are ineligible for jury service, including those with criminal convictions, people suffering severe mental disorder and members of the armed forces (see Criminal Justice Act 2003 for a complete list of exemptions).

It is for the jury to reach a verdict, by determining whether they are satisfied that the defendant is guilty beyond all reasonable doubt or innocent of the charges laid. They can ask the judge for advice but it is they who will make the final decision. The jury is told by the trial judge that they must base their decision upon the evidence put before them during the trial and not upon anything else, including things said outside the court or anything they may have read. The jury must therefore pay close attention to all the forms of evidence put before them. They must decide which facts they will accept from the evidence and which they will reject; what is true, what is false, what is mistaken and what is unreliable, and what weight should be placed upon the various parts of evidence put to them. Jurors must obey strict rules of confidentiality and not discuss their deliberations with anyone outside of their fellow jurors – either during the trial or afterwards – or risk being in contempt of court.

After the summing up by the judge, the jury will leave the courtroom to deliberate in private. A majority verdict of 10:2 is required, but jurors are free to make up their own minds, independent of other influences. There are some difficulties in ensuring that this independence of thought is protected, however, and a number of criticisms of jury decision making can be mounted, including:

- more dominant members of the jury may exert too much influence over deliberations and group dynamics on the jury might skew verdicts, based on factors other than the evidence;
- jurors' personal prejudices may influence their decision making;
- their lack of understanding of the law, the evidence and/or the judge's summing up may make it difficult for jurors to make an informed decision, particularly if they have not been able to follow the trial proceedings properly;
- the influence of 24/7 media reporting and jurors' access to information about cases may affect decision making.

In addition to these concerns, practical issues, such as the cost of jury trials, also come into play in debates about how justice might be provided.

Miscarriages of justice

Miscarriages of justice can occur throughout the criminal justice process: for example, through intimidation or mistreatment of suspects; or through misuse, fabrication or non-disclosure of important evidence. Examinations of miscarriages of justice tend to focus on those which take place in the Crown Court in front of a jury. To some degree, this is reasonable, given that these are the most serious cases and therefore the implications of a miscarriage are also very serious, as innocent people risk losing their liberty for many years. However, given that around 80% of criminal cases are dealt with in the magistrates' courts, such an emphasis on the Crown Court may shelter the magistrates' courts from the public's and the media's gaze when examining miscarriages. Thus, the risk of miscarriages occurring at magistrates' courts can be overlooked.

At magistrates' courts, most evidence comes directly from the police, and magistrates can be strongly disposed to believe in the police and in the veracity of their evidence. This can lead to concerns that at the magistrates' courts there is a risk that the burden of proof is reversed, with the defendant having to prove his or her innocence, rather than the prosecution prove their guilt – perhaps with no (or poor) legal representation. Furthermore, there are no transcripts of trials at magistrates' courts, which makes scrutiny of procedures more difficult.

At the Crown Court, miscarriages of justice can occur because of overdependence on forensic or expert evidence. In these cases, the scientific tests can be inaccurate, unreliable or badly carried out, or the expert witnesses' opinions can be taken as fact and not challenged or disputed effectively by the defence. For example, several cases involving women convicted of killing their children have highlighted the unquestioning over-reliance on expert evidence in court (see Box 5.2).

Box 5.2: Expert testimony and miscarriages of justice

Sally Clark was released on appeal in January 2003, having served three years of a life sentence following her conviction in 1999 for smothering 11-week-old Christopher in 1996 and for shaking eight-week-old Harry to death two years later. She has always maintained that her sons died of cot death syndrome.

Angela Cannings was released in December 2004, having served 20 months of a life sentence after being found guilty of smothering two of her babies: seven-week-old Jason in 1991 and 18-week-old Matthew in 1999. Mrs Cannings always insisted that her sons were victims of sudden infant death syndrome, which had killed her first child, Gemma, at the age of 13 weeks in 1989.

Evidence from one prosecution expert, the paediatrician Professor Sir Roy Meadow, was a key factor in each case. The judges who overturned Mrs Clark's conviction on appeal described Professor Meadow's evidence as 'manifestly wrong' and 'grossly misleading' – particularly the use in the trial of a statistic putting the chance of two babies in the same family suffering cot death at one in 73 million. Sally Clark died of alcohol poisoning in 2007, clearly indicating that a successful appeal does not always guarantee a happy ending in these types of cases.

In Mrs Cannings' case, the court was told again that Professor Meadow's evidence was misleading and in future his testimony would need a 'health warning' attached to it. On appeal, Professor Meadows was successful in overturning his striking from the medical register, as it was considered that he had given this evidence in good faith, using what scientific evidence was available at the time. During Mrs Cannings' appeal, fresh evidence from a geneticist, Professor Michael Patton, suggested that an undiscovered genetic disorder could have been responsible for the deaths of Jason and Matthew. He revealed that Mrs Cannings' great-grandmother and grandmother had both lost babies in unexplained circumstances and the daughter of a half-sister had suffered an 'acute life-threatening event'. Professor Patton said the new evidence – combined with details revealed in the original trial – 'strongly supported a genetic case for the infant deaths'.

For further details of this and other similar cases go to https://innocent.org.uk/

Further problems at the Crown Court can occur if the judge is seen to favour the prosecution evidence over that of the defence. The judge's job is to act as impartial adjudicator – but sometimes in their summing up to the jury or in their directions to the jury, they can lead the jury unfairly to a conviction. In addition, the quality of the defence's work can be poor. However, in order to overturn a conviction, a defendant must prove that their defence counsel was 'flagrantly incompetent', which allows considerable room for poor-quality representation without recourse to complaint for the defendant.

Appeals

Appeals from the magistrates' courts are heard in the Crown Court. The case will be fully reheard before a judge and two professional magistrates who took no part in the original trial. This process is only available to defendants who pleaded not guilty at their original trial.

From the Crown Court, appeals will be heard at the Court of Appeal. The right to appeal is available regardless of the original plea and a defendant can appeal against conviction or sentence.

The most common reasons to appeal a case include:

- improper exclusion or admission of evidence
- incorrect jury instructions
- lack of sufficient evidence to support a finding of guilty
- sentencing errors
- false arrest
- juror misconduct

- prosecutorial misconduct
- ineffective assistance of counsel.

Getting cases to the Court of Appeal is a difficult process, particularly if a defendant cannot interest a defence lawyer in their case or cannot afford the costs involved. Often they will have to rely on friends or family publicising their case and it being picked up by the media, in order to get an appeal moving. An appeal is normally made on the grounds that the original conviction was in some way unsafe.

Once all avenues for individual appeal have been followed, it is the role of the Criminal Cases Review Commission (CCRC) to review cases of those who believe they have been wrongly convicted or unfairly sentenced. It does not consider whether someone is guilty or innocent, however, but rather scrutinises new evidence or arguments that may cast doubt on the original verdict or sentence. Between 1997 and 2017, the CCRC received a total of 22,695 applications (including all ineligible cases) and completed 21,678 cases. Up to August 2017, the CCRC had referred 634 cases for appeal:

- of the 626 cases where appeals have been heard by the court, 419 appeals have been allowed and 194 dismissed;[2]
- 638 cases are still under review;
- 380 are awaiting review.

If an appeal is dismissed, it is possible to appeal to the Supreme Court. However, this is only possible if the case involves a point of law of general public importance. In other words, the ruling in the case may affect many cases in the future.

Once all national options are exhausted, there are two European courts that can engage with issues of the criminal law: the European Court of Justice and the European Court of Human Rights. Individuals can petition the European Court of Human Rights, if they think their human rights have been breached through their treatment by the criminal justice system. The European Court of Justice does not deal with individuals in this way, but can give rulings on the interpretation of UK criminal law; however, this would only be done if a UK court itself made such a referral. However, it is likely that these European-based options will no longer be available to British citizens following Brexit; and, as yet, there is no indication what, if anything, will replace them.

Focus on ... diversity in the judiciary

It is generally agreed that those working in the criminal justice professions should broadly reflect the society they police, prosecute and sentence. There are at least four reasons underlying this argument:

- First, it is thought that society will have more respect and trust of a justice system run by people like them and will feel more confident of receiving fair treatment.
- Second, it is considered that in a democracy we should be judged by equals, not by those from a narrow section of society.
- Third, it is thought that different groups in society see the world in different ways, so that women and/or ethnic minorities can improve and enrich the decision-making processes by offering a variety of perspectives.
- Fourth, it is argued that an understanding of, and ability to deal appropriately with, diversity issues strengthens the decision making of criminal justice agents, and thus those agents should be recruited from a wide range of backgrounds and cultures.

To improve diversity, several barriers to recruitment must be overcome, including the perception that criminal justice agencies are (institutionally) racist and dominated by a white, male culture, where the promotion prospects of both women and/or BAME staff are poor. In this section, we focus on diversity issues within the judiciary, to exemplify these interrelated issues further.

Annual judicial diversity statistics[3] provide an overview of the workforce, revealing evidence that the judiciary does indeed reflect a somewhat narrow slice of society: most of the 3,202 judges are male (72%) and white (95%) and over 50 years of age (86%). The number of female judges has gradually increased year on year, with 22% of court judges being women in 2011 compared to 28% in 2016. In addition, 51% of judges aged under 40 are women, compared with 16% of judges aged over 60, which suggests that the overall percentage of female judges will increase over time. The proportion of judges from BAME groups in 2016 was only 5%. However, a greater representation of BAME judges under 40 (8%), compared with 3% of those aged over 60, again suggests some improvement in these rates over time. Nearly three quarters (71%) of senior judges attended independent schools, compared to 7% of the general population; and 75% attended the Universities of Oxford or Cambridge, compared to less than 1% of the population.

The obvious solution to the diversity crisis in the judiciary is to recruit more female and BAME candidates. However, there are three main barriers to this strategy.

A legacy of mistrust

First, historic recruitment processes have created a legacy of mistrust about the way judges are appointed. Until 2006, judges were appointed through a system of 'soundings', where individuals were recommended for promotion rather than actively applying for this role. It was widely held that this rather secretive and archaic system led to a self-perpetuating cycle of recruitment, whereby existing judiciary simply recommended and appointed those who were 'like them'.

In 2006, the Judicial Appointments Commission (JAC) was established to select candidates through an open recruitment process. Judicial diversity statistics (discussed earlier) suggest that the JAC has improved diversity, particularly among women.

A lack of eligible candidates

Second, the JAC has argued that its efforts to improve diversity are hampered by the lack of eligible candidates from within the legal profession, and therefore it depends on the recruitment of students into law degrees and their career opportunities once qualified. Data from the Law Society (representing solicitors) and the Bar Council (representing barristers)[4] highlight some of the challenges faced in developing diversity through appointment: for example, statistics show that there is interest among women and BAME groups in studying law – women made up 67% and BAME students 36% of UK students starting a first degree law course in 2015. However, progress into the profession is more mixed: of the 6,077 individuals who qualified as solicitors in 2015, some 61% were women but only 13% were from BAME groups.

Overall, there were 168,226 solicitors on the roll in July 2015: of these, just over 50% were men and just under 50% were women. But only 12.5% were from BAME groups. These figures suggest that a significant proportion of BAME law students do not go on to pursue a career as a solicitor. Similarly, almost equal numbers of men (51%) and women (49%) were called to the Bar in 2014-15, with 35% of those called being from BAME groups.

Women do marginally better than men in terms of achieving tenancy, with 52% of those doing so being female. But the figures are more concerning for BAME groups, with only 14% of those achieving tenancy coming from this group – a substantial drop from those initially called to the Bar. At Queen's Counsel level – the most senior echelons of the Bar – the statistics show greater disproportionality, with only 15% of QCs being female in 2015 and only 7% from BAME groups.

Hence, there is evidence to support claims from the JAC that there is simply not an available pool of diverse candidates from which to select a more diverse judiciary. This suggests that the solutions lie within legal professions to ensure promotion and retention of women and BAME members (Neuberger, 2010).

Changing attitudes and beliefs

Third, attempts at reform of appointment processes and the promotion of equality policies by professional bodies provide the formal elements that are required to promote change, but without addressing underlying attitudes and beliefs, these formal policies can only have marginal impact. If those who might be eligible for judicial appointment simply do not apply, then the problem remains.

In 2013, the JAC published findings about attitudes towards judicial application from those eligible to apply (Judicial Appointments Commission, 2013). Some of its findings underline the extent of the barriers it faces in promoting greater diversity in the future:

- Although the JAC had a positive impact on overall perceptions of fairness in the judicial appointments process, 46% of respondents believed there is prejudice in the selection process.
- Among the factors that BAME respondents mentioned as increasing their likelihood of applying was more diverse role models.
- The perception that it is necessary to be a barrister, male, aged over 55, middle/upper class and Oxbridge educated was persistent among respondents.

Promoting diversity among criminal justice professions is one of the key responses to concerns over discrimination within the system. The example of judicial appointments highlights the need for widespread changes across recruitment to education, careers advice, institutional cultures and individual attitudes, if formal policy claims are to be realised.

Summary

■ The adversarial system used in criminal courts in England and Wales requires the prosecution to establish its case for a guilty verdict beyond reasonable doubt and therefore depends on the cross-examination of victims and witnesses, which can make it an intimidating and alien environment.

■ Justice is delivered through 330 magistrates' courts and 77 Crown Court centres across England and Wales. The number of courts has declined by 130 since 2010, and further closures are likely.

■ A two-tier court system separates less serious cases that are tried in the magistrates' courts from serious cases that are tried in a Crown Court, where a lay jury decides guilt.

■ The potential for miscarriages of justice exists across both court types, particularly regarding the way evidence is presented and the power of judges.

Guide to data sources and other online resources

Data used in this chapter is derived from the following sources

■ HMCTS annual reports and accounts provide most of the data relating to workloads, workforce and expenditure: https://www.gov.uk/government/publications/hm-courts-tribunals-service-annual-report-and-accounts-2015-to-2016

■ Specific data relating to the judicial workforce is available from the Courts and Tribunals Judiciary at: https://www.judiciary.gov.uk/publication-type/statisticsCriminal Justice Statistics provides a detailed breakdown of the number of offenders tried and sentenced at each of the courts, including information about outcomes and sentences: https://www.gov.uk/government/collections/criminal-justice-statistics

Other websites of interest

- Courts and Tribunals Judiciary: https://www.judiciary.gov.uk/about-the-judiciary
- Sentencing Council: https://www.sentencingcouncil.org.uk
- Criminal Cases Review Commission: www.ccrc.gov.uk
- Judicial Appointments Commission: https://jac.judiciary.gov.uk
- Law Society: https://www.lawsociety.org.uk
- Bar Council: www.barcouncil.org.uk

Taking it further ...

More in-depth reading about the issues raised in this chapter

Blackwell, S. and Seymour, F. (2015) Expert evidence and jurors' views on expert witnesses, *Psychiatry, Psychology and Law*, 22(5), 673-81

Neuberger, Baroness (2010) *Report of the Advisory Panel on Judicial Diversity*, London: Ministry of Justice.

Thomas, C. (2010) *Are juries fair?*, London: Ministry of Justice

Questions to consider from this chapter and your further reading

- Is the jury system the fairest way to decide the guilt of a defendant?
- Should jurors always believe 'expert' witness testimony?
- Is it just a question of time before we have a more diverse judiciary?

Notes

[1] A *juge d'instuction* is the judge or magistrate responsible for conducting the investigative hearing that precedes a criminal trial. In this hearing the major evidence is gathered and presented, and witnesses are heard and depositions taken.

[2] Statistics taken from https://ccrc.gov.uk/case-statistics/. The difference between the total number of CCRC referrals heard by the appeal courts and the number of outcomes recorded is accounted for by cases where the appeal proceedings have been heard but the judgment is awaited and a number of cases that were referred by the CCRC but the appeal was abandoned.

[3] The most recent statistics can be found at https://www.judiciary.gov.uk/about-the-judiciary/who-are-the-judiciary/diversity/judicial-diversity-statistics-2017/

[4] The statistics in this section are taken from www.barcouncil.org.uk/about-the-bar/facts-and-figures/statistics/ and www.barcouncil.org.uk/supporting-the-bar/equality-and-diversity/

SIX

The prison service

Background

Imprisonment is the most extreme form of punishment available to the court in the UK justice system and is widely used – the population in prison has not fallen below 80,000 since 2006. In fact, the rate of imprisonment in the UK is among the highest in western Europe, yet despite its apparent widespread use, prison remains a controversial method for dealing with offenders. The use of imprisonment as a form of punishment is not the focus of this chapter, but remains an important issue in the field of justice studies. Instead, this chapter deals with the organisation and delivery of the prison service in relation to the criminal justice system and therefore takes for granted the use of prison as a form of punishment. The latter is certainly not a given, however, and questions about whether we need prisons at all provide an important contribution to the more general debates about appropriate punishment.

Neither is it the case that imprisonment in the form that we currently know in England and Wales has a particularly long history. Prior to 1775, the vast majority of felons were transported to one of the colonies and imprisonment was used sparingly. As transportation became less available, the courts had little option but to increase prison sentences at home, leading to an explosion in prison numbers almost overnight. The consequent interest in imprisonment as a form of punishment should not be surprising, given the speed of change that the end to transportation generated. Victorian prisons were built to support particular principles about the purpose of prison as a form of moral reform, including solitude (small cells), silence (limited communal space) and hard labour (the treadmill).

The decades since the 1960s have witnessed the most significant shifts in prison policy and practice, including categorisation of prisons and prisoners according to risk and increasing concerns for security and containment following high-profile escapes. Prison riots in the 1990s, arising from prisoner discontent regarding the general conditions in prisons, led to some changes in practice as a result of the Woolf Report in 1991 (see the 'Key debates' section later in this chapter). However, political concern about the treatment of prisoners themselves is limited, compared to concerns about how to reduce the burden of cost of imprisoning so many offenders. Attempts at reducing the costs have given rise to a period of managerialism in the prison service that is similar to trends in other areas of the criminal justice system, most notably in the establishment of private contracts for prisons – a controversial issue to which we return later in this chapter.

Our discussion starts with an overview of the prison service, before going on to explore key issues around trends in imprisonment and overcrowding; and the related problems with prison conditions and the maintenance of order and security. It is fair to say that the majority of prisons are concerned with the needs of men – who make up around 96% of the total prison population. However, the particular issues raised with regard to women in prison make an important contribution to our understanding of equality in criminal justice, and this chapter ends with a more specific focus on women in prison.

1717 Transportation Act ⬥ **1779** Penitentiary Act ⬥ **1842** Pentonville Prison opened ⬥

Organisation and delivery

Since 2004, prison services in England and Wales have been delivered and commissioned together with probation services through Her Majesty's Prison and Probation Service (previously known as the National Offender Management Service – NOMS). In practice, this means responsibility for 107 public sector prisons and 14 'prisons under contract' (prisons managed by private sector companies).

The public sector prison service is managed through seven geographical regions, each of which is led by a deputy director. Separate 'functional' groups, each with its own 'director' operate across three areas: High Security, Young People, and Women.

The prison estate

The term 'estate' refers to the physical buildings that are used to house prisoners, although any sense that all prisons are built or designed in a similar way would be wrong. In fact, the estate is made up of a wide variety of buildings that range in size, age, types of prisoner held and security category.

The 'Prison Estate Transformation Programme', launched in 2010, has established clear aims for the prison estate, which are: to reduce costs, to improve the quality of accommodation, and to meet offenders' needs for work and to be kept closer to their homes. In practice, this has resulted in a shift from small, local prisons to larger prisons in urban areas.

Since 2010, a total of 12 prisons have closed, with a further five due to close, most of which were small prisons with under 300 inmates. Three new prisons have been commissioned, with a further four 'mini' prisons being built in existing sites. These new prisons are much larger than

1853 Penal Servitude Act ⟳ **1867** End of transportation ⟳

previous prisons and include Wrexham prison, described as Britain's first 'super-sized' prison with a capacity of 2,000.

Categories of prison and prisoners

Prisons are categorised according to function and security. This has implications for how the prison is run, including levels of security and the range and type of prisoner programmes that are provided. A further distinction is made between 'open' and 'closed' prisons. In an 'open' prison, prisoners are trusted to serve their sentence without trying to escape; they will have freedom of movement, they may have their own keys to their cells and may work outside the prison during the daytime. Open conditions like this might be used for prisoners who are coming to the end of their sentence as part of the process of resettlement. In closed prisons, inmates do not have these freedoms, and they are designed to hold prisoners securely, so that they cannot escape.

The current categorisation of prisons is as follows:

- **local prisons** – used for prisoners who are on remand awaiting trial (these are all closed prisons);
- **training prisons** – for sentenced prisoners; they provide programmes of work and/or education (they can be open or closed prisons);
- **high-security prisons** – used for sentenced prisoners who are deemed to be a security risk (all closed prisons);
- **women's prisons** – for adult female prisoners.

Prisoners are categorised according to the security risk they pose (of escaping from prison and harm to public should they do so):

- **Category A prisoners** – pose the highest risk of harm to public and risk of escape; always held in high-security prisons;
- **Category B prisoners** – may pose risk of harm or escape; may be held in high-security or closed training prison;

- **Category C prisoners** – pose limited risk of escape; held in closed training prison;
- **Category D prisoners** – risk of escape attempt is limited and harm to the public negligible; held in 'open' prison conditions.

These administrative classifications belie the depth and breadth of disadvantage exhibited by the prison population. Some of the most widely cited aspects of disadvantage are shown in Box 6.1, revealing a complex array of social, economic and health-related problems experienced by inmates.

Box 6.1: Social and economic aspects of disadvantage among the prison population

Among the prison population:

- 42% of prisoners have been expelled or permanently excluded from school;
- 51% of those entering prison had literacy skills expected of an 11 year old;
- 15% of newly sentenced prisoners were homeless before custody;
- 13% of prisoners have never had a job;
- 20-30% of people in prison are estimated to have a learning disability;
- 25% of women and 16% of men in prison reported symptoms of psychosis (in the population the rate is 4%);
- 64% of prisoners reported having used drugs in the four weeks before custody;38% of prisoners believe their alcohol drinking habits were a big problem.

Source: Prison Reform Trust, 2016

All prisons are funded by central government via the Ministry of Justice (MOJ) and their expenditure is reported through the National Prison and Probation Service annual accounts (formerly NOMS). Overall expenditure on NOMS fell from £4.1 billion in 2010-11 to £3.8 billion in 2015-16 – a reduction of 7%. Specific expenditure on prisons is not provided for 2010-11, but in 2015-16 public prison expenditure was £1.5 billion, and 9% of MOJ expenditure was used to fund private prisons (around £349 million).

Table 6.1 shows the cost per prison place for different categories of prison. The most expensive prison places are for young people, at £85,975 per year. The most widely used prison type – male category C provides the cheapest prison places, at £28,510 per year. Putting these figures into context helps us to think about whether these places represent value for money: the cost of one year's private education at Eton is £37,000 for a young person aged 15; and the average annual income in the UK is £26,500. Some might argue that the money spent keeping some people in prison, given recidivism rates, might be used

Table 6.1: Annual costs of prison per prisoner by prison function, 2015-16

Function	Average population	Overall resource expenditure (£)	Cost per prisoner (£)
Male Category B	6,327	205,659,080	32,503
Male Category C	32,001	912,342,083	28,510
Male dispersal	3,170	185,232,756	58,428
Female closed	588	22,026,147	37,449
Female local	2,753	128,350,235	46,613
Female open	187	8,257,214	44,235
Male closed YOI (ages 15-21)	2,158	111,725,719	51,761
Male YOI (ages 15-17)	546	46,970,916	85,975
Male local	32,345	996,935,296	30,822
Male open	4,629	129,479,835	27,972

to better effect in parts of the welfare system rather than in criminal justice.

As at March 2016, around 31,000 prison officers were employed in public prisons in England and Wales – the lowest number for at least 20 years. In 2000, there were 42,870 employees, rising to a peak of 51,060 in 2009. Public sector prison workforce statistics reveal that there were 14,000 fewer staff in 2015-16 than in 2010-11 – a 42% reduction. The trends for the period are shown in Figure 6.1.

Figure 6.1: Public sector prison staff in post at end of financial year 2010-11 to 2015-16

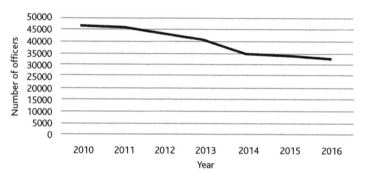

Prisons are staffed according to benchmarks, which identify the number of staff required to permit safe, decent and secure operating levels. In 2015-16 there was a shortfall of 6% (1,974 officers), with some areas at greater risk than others – most notably in London and the South East.

Prison population statistics give an overall picture of prison service workloads. Figure 6.2 shows average prison populations since 1900. There has been a 90% increase in the prison population since 1990 – giving some indication as to the pressures that the prison service faces in meeting demand.

1967 Criminal Justice Act ⮕ **1979** Report of the May Committee on the Prison Service ⮕

Figure 6.2: Prison population in England and Wales,[1] 1902-2012

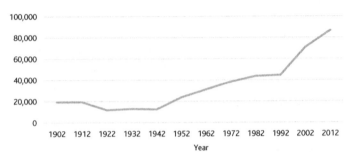

Note

[1] The prison population annual average is the average of the 12-month-end prison populations.

Functions and powers

Understanding the purpose of imprisonment and consequently the role of prisons is not straightforward, and in common with many of the agencies of the criminal justice is a matter of politics, ideology and philosophy. In particular, the aims and objectives of the prison service reflect a number of priorities that can conflict with each other, as we shall see.

We can conceive of prisons as an 'end point' in the criminal justice system by virtue of their punitive function – offenders are sentenced to prison as punishment for committing crime. Yet prisons also perform a 'coercive' function, where individuals are sent to prison because they have failed to comply with an existing court order; and a 'custodial' function, where accused individuals are held awaiting trial (commonly referred to as 'on remand'). In the latter case, prison is far from the 'end point' in the criminal justice system, but can occur immediately after someone is arrested. The position of individuals on remand is generally among the poorest of any prisoners in the system, since they have

1980 HM Inspectorate of Prisons introduced ⟲ **1982** Criminal Justice Act ⟲

restricted access to prison programmes of education or training and consequently end up spending more time locked in cells than many sentenced prisoners.

Thus, holding prisoners securely as a means of punishment and as means of protecting the public remains a core function for the prison service. The extent to which it is successful in doing so is most often represented by data relating to prison escapes, which remain extremely rare – only 1 to 2 per year.

The Gladstone Committee Report (1985) famously argued that prison *is* punishment not *for* punishment – in other words, prisoners should not experience further punishment while in prison – and, furthermore return to society 'better men [and women] than when they went in'. The pursuit of this aim continues and, in its present form, rehabilitation of offenders is organised around four main types of intervention:

- **education programmes** – designed to improve the life chances of offenders on release and increase the likelihood of successful reintegration into mainstream society (mainly through employment);
- **medical interventions** – designed to remove clinical conditions that might contribute to offending behaviour (most notably those relating to drug and alcohol use);
- **therapeutic interventions** – these are designed to encourage offenders to modify their behaviour by focusing on self-awareness and personal growth (for example for sex offenders or violent offenders);
- **employment opportunities** – designed to improve life chances on release, by giving prisoners work experience and the chance to learn new skills and to be productive.

However, good quality evidence relating to the effectiveness of any or all of these approaches to reform and rehabilitation is limited.

1990 Strangeways prison riots ◗ **1991** Woolf Report ◗

Furthermore, beyond a requirement for prisons to provide basic education provision, deciding what to provide and to whom remains in the hands of individual prison governors and thus provision across the prison system is inconsistent. In some prisons, programmes are only available to prisoners with good behaviour records – rehabilitation is therefore a 'reward'. The capacity for rehabilitation to be effective also depends on prisoner engagement: simply coping with prison life might limit offenders' capacity to engage with programmes. Prison is sometimes called a 'university of crime', where offenders might be more likely to learn new crime skills rather than life skills. There is also evidence that prisoners serving short sentences are least likely to be offered interventions – this might be because they are not in prison long enough to complete programmes or because priority is given to those serving longer sentences for more serious crimes.

A range of evidence can be used to question the effectiveness of rehabilitation and reform programmes in prison, most notably 'proven reoffending rates', which show the proportion of offenders who go on to receive a subsequent conviction in the 12 months following release. Figures from the Ministry of Justice show a consistent and persistent reoffending rate for adult offenders of 25%. However, variations in reoffending rates exist (see Box 6.2) between men (25.7%) and women (17.9%), and experiences of custody. The more times someone has served a custodial sentence, the more likely they are to reoffend; and the longer a custodial sentence is, the less likely someone is to reoffend.

Box 6.2: Selected reoffending rates, 2014-15

The proven re-offending rate for men was 25.7% and for women 17.9%

The proportion of offenders with no previous custodial sentences who reoffended was 16% compared with 68% of those with 11 or more previous custodial sentences.

The proportion of offenders who reoffend after a sentence of less than 12 months was 59.7% compared with 24% of those who served sentences of between 4 and 10 years.

Source: Ministry of Justice, 2017

The history of prison policy shows us that prison is expected to perform a range of functions simultaneously in ways that are appropriate to a very diverse prisoner population. Managing these expectations in perfect conditions would be difficult enough, but managing them in the context of pressures arising from budgetary constraints and differing political priorities is almost impossible.

Key debates

In this section, our focus is on three interrelated issues that highlight some of the complexity involved in managing the prison system. First, we consider trends in imprisonment that highlight the ever-growing prison populations worldwide and the pressures this brings to institutions in the form of overcrowding. Second, we consider conditions in prison and the way that these can undermine attempts to rehabilitate offenders – a situation that is exacerbated by increasing numbers of prisoners. Third, we explore the issue of security and order maintenance, to highlight the ways in which overcrowding and poor conditions can combine to generate insecurity in prison, and we consider the current policy reforms that attempt to deal with this crisis.

Trends in imprisonment

Given the previous discussion, it is of no surprise to learn that rising rates of imprisonment lie at the heart of many of the political, economic and moral debates about the capacity of prisons to fulfil their aims of providing both punishment and rehabilitation. Concerns over cost, security and conditions are all related to rising prison numbers, so understanding the nature of trends in imprisonment and how to interpret these is important.

In England and Wales, the prison population rose by 90% between 1990 and 2015 (see Figure 2.2 in Chapter Two), and although prisoner numbers have remained fairly stable since 2012, the overall size of the prison population continues to give rise to concerns about how the prison service can manage this population.

Trends in the numbers of people held in prison are important, because they give a sense of the overall capacity required within the prison system. By comparing the number of prisoners held in any institution against its 'Certified Normal Accommodation', we can assess levels of overcrowding. Table 6.2 shows the levels of overcrowding for the three most overcrowded and the three least overcrowded prisons at May 2016. The most overcrowded prisons are all male category B prisons – housing inmates who are deemed at some risk to the public. At the other end of the scale, the least overcrowded prisons are almost all young offender institutions. While the prison estate strategy has sought to address some of the criticisms levied at the prison system in terms of location of prisons and quality of accommodation, it has failed to confront the key issue of overcrowding. Cell-sharing remains one of the strategies used by the prison service to maintain capacity

– despite this being in contravention of UN Standard Minimum Rules for the Treatment of Prisoners (to be discussed later in this chapter).

Table 6.2: Levels of overcrowding in selected establishments, May 2016

Establishment	Category	In use CNA[1]	Population	% population to CNA
Kennet	Category C (closed 2017)	175	329	188.0%
Leeds	Category B	669	1,138	170.1%
Wandsworth	Category B	943	1,600	169.7%
Downview	Female	130	87	66.9%
Cookham Wood	YOI	188	140	74.5%
Deerbolt	YOI	513	391	76.2%

Source: MOJ Prison Population Bulletin, May 2016, available online at: https://www.gov.uk/government/collections/prison-population-statistics

Note: [1] CNA is certified normal accommodation.

The most widely accepted explanation for the increase in prison population numbers is that the courts are passing more severe sentences, reflecting a general 'punitive turn' in criminal justice politics since the 1980s (see Chapter One).

However, the number of people in prison is also a reflection of general population trends, and so analysts use the 'incarceration rate' to compare prison populations over time and between countries. The incarceration rate calculates the number of people in prison per 100,000 of the population. World Prison Briefings show that in 1990 the incarceration rate for England and Wales was 90 per 100,000; in 2016, this had risen to 146 per 100,000. Table 6.3 shows incarceration rates for a selection of countries ranked from highest to lowest. The US and Russia have historically topped these rankings worldwide, but

England and Wales come highest in comparisons of western European countries, where the median rate of incarceration is 84.

Table 6.3: Incarceration rate (per 100,000 population) for selected countries[a]

Country	Incarceration rate
Sweden	53
Finland	57
Denmark	59
Netherlands	61
Norway	74
Germany	76
Ireland	81
Switzerland	83
Greece	89
Italy	92
France	101
Canada	114
Spain	129
Portugal	135
Scotland	138
England and Wales	146
Jordan	150
Saudi Arabia	161
Russia	433
USA	666

Source: *World Prison Briefings* (2017)

Note: The World Prison Brief collects the latest available data from a range of countries, but not necessarily from the same date. Details for each country can be found on the World Prison Brief website: www.prisonstudies.org

Aside from the sheer size of the prison population, the social characteristics of prisoners shown in Box 6.1 earlier provide further evidence of the nature and scale of the difficulties that prison officers face in managing the balance between security and rehabilitation.

Conditions in prison

Conditions inside prisons matter, because they can support or undermine more general objectives for the prison service. We have already seen that the punitive function of prison might support relatively poor prison conditions: the principle of 'less eligibility', wherein conditions inside prison should be no better than the worst living conditions in mainstream society to ensure that prisoners do not experience any form of 'luxury' while serving their sentence. In contrast, it is widely argued that poor prison conditions can affect individuals' response to rehabilitation and simply reinforce a perception of them as 'irredeemable'. In addition, poor prison conditions can generate grievances among prisoners that can lead to disturbances and riots that undermine safety and security for prisoners and staff.

A question is immediately raised about relative conditions in prison – or what might be deemed appropriate conditions for prison. The *United Nations Standard Minimum Rules for the Treatment of Prisoners* (the *Nelson Mandela Rules*) (UNODC, 2015) runs to 122 specific rules that give an indication about what prisons *should* be like and provide a benchmark against which we might be able to compare prison conditions across countries, but tell us little about what is deemed appropriate in our own prison system. Instead, we can draw on prison inspectorate reports from Her Majesty's Inspectorate of Prisons for England and Wales (HMI Prisons), which offer insight into conditions that continue to persist in some UK prisons.

HMIP reports focus on four areas of prison life, each of which contributes to a sense of the overall condition of a prison and the general priorities that the service as a whole seeks to achieve:

- **safety** – prisoners, particularly the most vulnerable, are held safely;
- **respect** – prisoners are treated with respect for their human dignity;

- **purposeful activity** – prisoners are able, and expected, to engage in activity that is likely to benefit them;
- **resettlement** – prisoners are prepared for their release back into the community and effectively helped to reduce the likelihood of reoffending.

On an individual basis, prisons are ranked by inspectors on a scale between 1 and 4 (with 1 being the weakest) and an annual report by HMIP draws out the most important findings from inspections for any particular year. These reports and the overall prison performance statistics provide a snapshot of the state of the prison service at any one time. Themes recur and the problems of violence, problematic drug use and suicide levels in prison reflect both patterns of disadvantage that inmates experience before they arrive in prison and the limited coping strategies inmates have to deal with the pressures of being in prison.

Furthermore, the reality of life inside prison may undermine efforts at individual rehabilitation because prison life, and the ways people might need to act in order to cope, is very different to mainstream society. For example, inmates do not need to pay bills or do laundry or cook or shop for themselves, so they might question the value of learning everyday skills.

Box 6.3: The Woolf Report

In 1990, a riot by inmates at Strangeways prison led to the Woolf Report (1991), which has been described as the most influential inquiry into prisons since Gladstone in 1895. Woolf argued that there were three requirements for prison stability (which should reduce disturbances and riots in future):

- **security** – to prevent prisoners escaping;
- **control** – of prisoners to prevent disruption;

■ **justice** – towards prisoners to prepare them for return to society.

Woolf was instrumental in subsequent changes to prison conditions. Among the 204 recommendations included in his report, Woolf precipitated an end to the controversial practice of 'slopping out', where prisoners were unable to use toilet facilities during the night and were forced to use open buckets, which they then had to empty and clean out in the morning. However, it is widely accepted that despite improvements, pressures on the prison system emanating from increasing numbers of prisoners undermine the positive impact that Woolf's recommendations may have had.

Maintaining order

Achieving policy objectives means that prisons need to be secure and prisoners need to be controlled. The ultimate breakdown in prison order would be prison riots – and there is not a decade of the period since the Gladstone report in 1895 when prison riots have not occurred. Riots are an extreme example of the breakdown of order, however. It is also important to understand more mundane issues about maintaining order on a daily basis, because it is these issues that may affect individuals' experience of prison, and ultimately whether prison can be defined as 'safe', and conducive, therefore, to attempts at rehabilitation.

Understanding the causes of disorder in prison go some way to indicating where policy priorities might be focused. Three issues are most commonly discussed: overcrowding, complex needs of prisoners, and staff shortages. Overcrowding affects all aspects of prison life, from cancelled free time for prisoners because staff cannot manage numbers, to meal times being disrupted when there are simply too many people to feed in a given time period and not enough places available in work or training programmes. Ultimately, overcrowding generates grievances for prisoners that can spill over into protest. The composition of prison populations, and the multiple problems individuals may bring with them to prison (including mental health problems, histories of violence, and so on), generates pressures on staff and the system to provide appropriate interventions. When combined with overcrowding, this population may be extremely difficult to control. Finally, staff shortages reinforce all the difficulties identified here, both in terms of lack of capacity within the system to provide services and the consequences of rising levels of violence on staff themselves.

Table 6.4: Assaults and self-inflicted deaths in prison, 2010-11 and 2015-16

	2010-11	2015-16
All assault incidents	14,915	22,195
Assaults in male prisons	14,280	21,368
Assaults in female prisons	635	827
All self-inflicted deaths in prison	63	105
– self-inflicted deaths in male prisons	60	94
– self-inflicted deaths in female prisons	3	11

Source: Safety in custody statistics (MOJ)

The evidence that order is threatened in UK prisons is hard to refute. It includes increasing levels of violence within prison, and increasing rates of self-inflicted deaths (see Table 6.4). In addition, concerns about the supply of illegal drugs in prison have been exacerbated by the increase in use of new psychoactive substances, particularly synthetic cannabinoids such as Spice.

One of the key mechanisms used in the prison system to maintain order is the Incentives and Earned Privileges scheme, introduced in 1995. The scheme rewards good behaviour, by providing additional benefits to prisoners, which can be removed if necessary. Currently the scheme comprises four levels: 'entry level' is applied to all newly convicted prisoners who, once they have completed the requirements at this level and are considered to be behaving well and engaging in rehabilitation programmes can be moved to 'standard level'. A lower 'basic' level is used for prisoners who have behaved badly or not engaged in rehabilitation, while an 'enhanced' level exists for those who behave well and engage for a minimum of three months.

Prison governors have discretion about the way the scheme is implemented locally, but all prisons are required to include the following six 'designated key earnable privileges':

- extra and improved visits;
- eligibility to earn higher rates of pay;
- access to in-cell TV;
- opportunity to wear own clothes;
- access to private cash;
- time out of cell for association.

As an example of how the privileges system operates: at the point of entry, most prisoners are eligible for two visits per month for one hour each, and might have access to in-cell television with restricted channels – but they would not be allowed to wear their own clothes. After around four weeks, they might move to a 'standard' level of privileges and be allowed their own clothes, for example – but some luxury items would still be unavailable, such as pillows, curtains, games consoles or musical instruments.

In theory, the scheme provides flexibility for prison staff to reward those prisoners who are well behaved, but in practice the 'enhancements' available can be restricted by lack of staff to supervise or organise additional association time or increased visits, for example. Most controversially, changes introduced in 2013 included a ban on prisoners receiving parcels from outside the prison, including books and other personal items. It has been argued that the ban prevented prisoners from maintaining positive contact with friends and family that could undermine aspects of rehabilitation and resettlement (see Chapter Seven).

Focus on ... women in prison

The differential treatment of women compared to men throughout the criminal justice system has long been a cause for debate. Some argue that women are treated more leniently than men (the 'chivalry thesis') by virtue of their female status; others believe that the system is harsher in its treatment of women, whose criminality is perceived as a betrayal of femininity. These debates place women in contrast to men and can often ignore wider questions about the needs of women in particular. Consequently, it has been suggested that treating women the same as men is not always appropriate. The Corston Report (Home Office, 2007) was instrumental in establishing the principle that the complex needs of female offenders meant that equal treatment could lead to unequal outcomes and that consequently differential treatment was necessary. The focus in this section is on women in prison, where aspects of both 'equal treatment' and 'different responses' debates can be discerned.

Criminal justice statistics provide a range of evidence comparing women's and men's treatment throughout the system. Two areas are of particular interest in terms of the impact they have on our understanding of how and why women are in prison. First, there is a raft of evidence to show different offending profiles between men and women, which can result in perverse outcomes for imprisonment: 84% of women served sentences for non-violent offences in 2016, compared to 76% for men. Women are more likely to be sentenced for theft than for violent offences, and a significant proportion of theft offences relate to shoplifting (80% in 2015). A high proportion of women in prison are serving sentences as a result of prosecutions brought from outside the criminal justice system, including TV licence evasion, welfare fraud, and so on. These prosecutions are not eligible for out-of-court disposals (warnings or cautions), because they are not subject to arrest by the police. Consequently, the process of prosecution can lead to unequal sentencing outcomes for women compared to men, who are more likely to be dealt with by the criminal justice system.

Second, evidence shows differences in sentencing patterns (in large part reflecting less serious offending), where many more women receive short sentences compared to men. In 2015-16, 63% of women were sentenced for six months or less, compared to 47% of men. This makes the impact of prison much harsher overall, as it reduces the opportunity for women to participate in rehabilitative programmes.

Women make up around 5% of the total prison population and only 10 prisons are reserved for female prisoners. The average female prison population at December 2016 was 3,885, down from 4,236 in December 2011. However, there are around 8,000 prison receptions in female prisons in any one year. It is useful to compare the prison population data with receptions, which can give a clearer picture of the number of women who may have been sent to prison, even for very short periods: for the year ending December 2015 there were 8,490 receptions to female prisons.

The overwhelmingly male dominance of the prison system has meant that the needs of women in custody have frequently been hidden. Policy is most often concerned with the issues that dominate in the male estate, such as violence or security, rather than those that affect women prisoners. Yet a range of data shows that women who enter prison have different needs to men, and that the impact of female imprisonment is also different to that of men, particularly in terms of the ripple effect on children and families (see Box 6.4). While the number of children affected by female imprisonment is not known – estimates vary from 2,000 (MOJ, 2015b) to 17,000 (Wilks-Wiffen, 2011) – evidence of the impact of separation is much clearer, particularly with regard to high rates of self-harming and self-inflicted deaths among the female prison population. This is partly attributed to the problems associated with maintaining relationships with children in prison. A key factor lies with the organisation of the prison estate: as there are relatively few women's prisons, prison visits are expensive and difficult for family members to organise. Furthermore, most women do not have homes to go to when they are released, and they are less likely than men to have a job when they leave prison.

Box 6.4: Impact of imprisonment on children

- **Disruption to children's lives** – the Prison Reform Trust estimates that only around 5% of children whose mothers are in prison stay in their own homes.
- **Breakdown in contact** – children lose contact with mothers in prison partly as a result of the geographic dispersion of female prisons.
- **Social costs** – children's long-term wellbeing is compromised by the effects of poverty and homelessness that may arise on a mother's release from prison, and parental imprisonment is a known risk factor for the onset of criminal behaviour in young people.

Responses to the needs of female offenders most often call into question the need for custodial sentences and focus on alternatives to prison for women. Prominent among these responses has been the development of Women's Community Services (WCS) that provide community-based facilities for female offenders. During 2006, Baroness Corston undertook a review of vulnerable women in the criminal justice system following the deaths of six women in Styal Prison. The Corston Report was published in 2007 (Home Office, 2007) and remains a landmark report in relation to the treatment of women. Among 43 recommendations, the report called for the expansion of women's centres as an alternative to custody for women offenders. Since then, a network of women's centres has been established across England and Wales, providing probation services including management of community sentences alongside support provision such as education, training, counselling and advice to female offenders and those at risk of offending. This holistic approach to female offending has been widely supported – including core funding from the MOJ to expand services across the country.

However, despite the significant influence of Baroness Corston's report, in recent years there appears to have been a loss of momentum in terms of implementing her recommendations. The women's prison population has not significantly reduced, perhaps partly because Corston's vision of women's community centres as viable alternatives to custody has not been fully realised. Indeed, the holistic gender-specific work done by these centres is now at risk from the new privatisation of probation services (see Chapter Seven), a process which threatens the secure and long-term funding for such services and has also prevented their expansion as recommended by Corston (Women in Prison, 2017). The focus on 'reoffending' as the primary measure of success under 'Transforming Rehabilitation', is at odds with the holistic approach taken by women's centres, where 'distance travelled' by all the women they work with is seen as a greater measure of success than reducing reoffending for a smaller number of those who already have a criminal record.

In addition, Corston's recommendation that the women's custodial estate be replaced with small, geographically dispersed custodial centres seems as far away today as it did in 2007. There is concern that the proposed community prisons for women will simply be tagged on to existing male prisons and thus will not focus on a gender-specific service which properly recognises the differential treatment that might better assist women prisoners with their complex needs.

Summary

- The modern prison system dates from the 19th century, although the decades since the 1960s have witnessed considerable changes in policy and practice.
- The prison estate comprises a mix of 'public' and 'private' prisons. The largest prison in England and Wales is Wrexham (2,000 prisoners).
- Prisons are categorised by function and prisoners by security risk, leading to a complex set of administrative classifications.
- Prison is the most extreme form of punishment available in England and Wales, although it is required to perform a dual function: to punish and to rehabilitate offenders. While the punishment function of prison is achieved through deprivation of liberty, the reform function is much more difficult to define, measure or achieve.
- Rising prison populations generate pressure on the system that can lead to overcrowding and resultant deterioration in conditions that might lead to disturbances or riots and undermine attempts at rehabilitation.

Guide to data sources and other online resources

Data used in this chapter is derived from the following sources

- Prison population statistics are produced weekly: https://www.gov.uk/government/collections/prison-population-statistics
- Prison Reform Trust 'Bromley Briefings': www.prisonreformtrust.org.uk/Publications/Factfile

- Cost of prison places forms part of Prison and Performance statistics from the MOJ: https://www.gov.uk/government/collections/prison-and-probation-trusts-performance-statistics
- NOMS annual reports and accounts for expenditure: https://www.gov.uk/government/publications/noms-annual-report-and-accounts-2015-2016
- NOMS workforce statistics for details of staffing: https://www.gov.uk/government/collections/national-offender-management-service-workforce-statistics
- Proven reoffending statistics produced by the MOJ: https://www.gov.uk/government/collections/proven-reoffending-statistics
- Safety in custody statistics: https://www.gov.uk/government/collections/safety-in-custody-statistics
- World Prison Brief: www.prisonstudies.org

Other websites of interest

- Her Majesty's Inspectorate of Prisons for England and Wales (HMIP) provides reports about individual prison inspections as well as thematic reviews of issues in prison: https://www.justiceinspectorates.gov.uk/hmiprisons
- *United Nations Standard Minimum Rules for the Treatment of Prisoners (the Nelson Mandela Rules)* (United Nations Office on Drugs and Crime): https://www.unodc.org/documents/justice-and-prison-reform/GA-RESOLUTION/E_ebook.pdf

Taking it further ...

More in-depth reading about the issues raised in this chapter

DR. and Robson, J. (2016) *A matter of conviction: A blueprint for community-based rehabilitative prisons*, London: RSA

Women in Prison (2017) *Corston +10: The Corston Report 10 years on. How far have we come on the road to reform for women affected by the criminal justice system?*, London: Women in Prison

Questions to consider from this chapter and your further reading

- What should the purpose of prison be?
- Should we send fewer people to prison?
- Should women be treated differently than men in prison?

SEVEN

The probation service

Background

From its roots in the Victorian temperance movement[1] to its contemporary focus on managing offenders in the community, the probation service has always played an unusual, albeit crucial, role in the criminal justice system. In fact, the genesis of the service arose out of the establishment of a new form of sentencing – the 'Probation Order' – in 1907, which created a formal role for probation officers to supervise offenders in the community in cases where the court felt a prison sentence was not necessary.

Reading the history of the probation service, it is difficult not to be struck by a sense of continual change and crisis in both its aims and its role within the justice system. In its early days, officers were criticised for their lack of professionalism (arising in part from the fact that the service had been almost wholly voluntary and missionary until 1912). In the post-1945 period, probation officers saw their remit expanded to include the supervision of released prisoners. By the 1950s, the service was wholly professional, influential in the criminal justice system and responsible for the supervision of 4,500 offenders, 4,000 children in need of care and protection, and 7,000 ex-prisoners.

The 1960s saw probation officers begin to work in prisons and, in 1965 'Aftercare' was added to the name of the Probation Service, reflecting its new role in supervising released prisoners. This was particularly important following the Criminal Justice Act 1967, which established parole for the first time and thus the concept of released prisoners being placed on licence and under supervision. Through the subsequent decade, the probation service continued to develop its practices to include treatment models using techniques such as group work and cognitive behavioural therapy and the provision of services aimed at reforming offenders through a casework approach that recognised both social causes and individual characteristics that contributed to offending behaviour.

However, since the 1970s onwards, it is fair to say that there has been a seismic shift both in terms of the respect in which the probation service was held and its traditional way of working. The so-called 'nothing works' era of the 1980s saw the role of probation change significantly, as a more punitive turn in criminal justice policy shifted the role of the probation service away from rehabilitation towards offender management, punishment in the community and public protection.

Aside from these shifts in the practice of probation work, the organisation itself has undergone enormous changes since its inception, from local probation services that were relatively independent to an almost entirely privatised model of provision in 2017, based on national priorities. It is not difficult to understand why probation officers have, at times, felt under siege and undervalued for the work that they undertake.

In fact, in 2017 it might seem a little strange to devote a whole chapter of a short guide to criminal justice to the probation service, when it seems to have almost disappeared from mainstream public sector provision. However, such a view risks missing an important element in the criminal justice process – namely, the continuing importance of offender supervision in the community and the provision of post-release services. The history of the probation service also reveals how much the political and professional landscape of criminal justice has changed in the past 100 years and, perhaps, gives an indication about the possible direction of future developments.

In common with preceding chapters, this discussion begins by describing the current organisational features of the probation service, before exploring key debates about the management of high-risk offenders in the community and the implications of privatising the management of low- to medium-risk offenders. A final section explores the challenges that probation services face in supporting ex-prisoners' resettlement, where the limits of the criminal justice system to address the social circumstances of offenders becomes increasingly clear.

Organisation and delivery

Probation services provide statutory provision across six key areas: court services; community supervision; custody; work with victims; management of approved premises; and youth offending services. In doing so, probation officers work with offenders from conviction through to resettlement in the community and form a key part of the 'end-to-end' management of offenders that is designed to support reductions in reoffending. The challenges specific to resettlement are discussed in the 'Focus on ...' section at the end of this chapter.

These wide-ranging services are currently provided through two main organisational frameworks: the National Probation Service (NPS) and community rehabilitation companies (CRCs). At a local level, 21 independent CRCs operate across geographical areas aligned with local authority boundaries – effectively privatising around 70% of probation work with medium- to low-risk offenders in the community. The implications of this is discussed in more detail in the 'Key debates' section of this chapter. The NPS forms part of Her Majesty's Prison and

1973 Community service introduced ➲ **1974** Robert Martinson publishes his study 'what works' ➲

Probation Service (HMPPS),[2] and is organised into six regional 'divisions', with services provided through local delivery unit clusters that are also aligned with local authority boundaries.

In common with prisons, probation services are funded by central government via the Ministry of Justice (MOJ) and their expenditure is reported through HMPPS accounts. This expenditure is split between the NPS and the funding provided to CRCs. In 2015-16, the NPS expenditure was £412 million and the cost of CRCs was 12% of total National Offender Management Service (NOMS)[3] expenditure (around £466 million). The changes to probation service organisation mean that there is no comparable data to consider overall trends at this time.

Probation service workloads are dependent on the volume and types of sentences that are handed down from the courts as well as political imperatives. In the past, these shifts may have had workload implications for those working in the probation service, but under the new funding model there are significant implications for the new CRCs, whose funding relies on the volume of cases they handle. Table 7.1 outlines the number of new start cases managed by the NPS and CRCs.

For the period October 2015 to September 2016, the NPS was responsible for 90% of the new starts in probation. This has meant that the volume of cases handled by the new CRCs is considerably less than originally estimated. The explanation for this imbalance lies with the increasing volume of serious cases coming through the courts, but the implications are: reduced funding for the new CRCs; and increased workload for the NPS.

At court, around 1,800 probation officers are responsible for preparing pre-sentence assessments and reports, and delivering bail accommodation and support services for 371 courts around the country. The court services team prepare around 150,000 pre-sentence reports each year, and work with around 50,000 offenders. Community

1991 Criminal Justice Act ➲ **1992** Introduction of national standards for probation service ➲

Table 7.1: Probation new-starts, October 2015 to September 2016

	Total new-starts	Proportion CRC	Proportion NPS
All court orders	139,810	6%	94%
All pre- and post-release supervision	101,460	15%	85%

Source: *Offender Management Statistics Quarterly* (NOMS)

supervision forms a large proportion of probation work, working with the most high-risk offenders. This work represents 40% of NPS costs, reflecting the staff-intensive nature of the work. Under the new NPS operating model, community supervision is based on an individual casework approach, using one-to-one supervision as the best-evidenced model to support desistance from crime.

While in custody, prisoners are also under the supervision of the probation service either for pre-release work or parole assessments, for example. Once released, some offenders will be moved to approved premises that are also managed by the NPS. Approved premises provide accommodation that allows offenders to be supervised in the community when other accommodation might be unsuitable. The NPS manages 89 approved premises, providing 2,000 bed spaces. Probation officers can be seconded to work with Youth Offending Services within local authorities, and are also responsible for work with victims of violent and sexual offences, specifically to provide information about offenders and sentences and to support victims in preparing victim personal statements.

Two themes have become central to understanding the organisation and delivery of probation services in recent years: the division of responsibility between NPS and CRC staff; and the ongoing emphasis on risk assessment. The functions of CRC staff are more limited than those of NPS probation officers; only probation officers employed by

1999 Publication of 'What Works? Reducing reoffending: Evidence based practice'

the NPS prepare court reports on offenders and thus carry out the early assessment of any risk they pose and any recommendation for suitable interventions or sentences. These probation officers also carry out the Case Allocation System, which assesses whether an offender should be supervised by the NPS or by a CRC. In order to make this decision, NPS probation officers are responsible for completing a Risk of Serious Harm screening and calculating a Risk of Serious Recidivism score in addition to the standard OASys procedure (see Table 7.2 later in this chapter). Thus, the classification of risk and the allocation of cases remain firmly in the public sector domain.

Historically, the probation service employed around 16,000 probation officers, but the new organisational arrangements since 2014 have seen the workforce split. At March 2016, the NPS workforce total was 9,631, of which three quarters (75.4%) were female. Around 7,000 staff transferred to the CRCs in June 2014, but workforce diversity data is not available for these organisations. CRCs are in control of their own staffing levels, with the MOJ having no control over the numbers employed or the quality of the workforce. In contrast, the NPS runs programmes of training, leading to the Professional Qualification in Probation (PQiP), which qualifies individuals as probation officers. The NPS also employs probation service officers in more junior positions that do not require graduate-level qualifications. These changes to probation service training are in part a response to the need for more officers as workloads have risen – an issue to which we return in the subsequent discussion.

Function and powers

The objective of the NPS is: 'to protect the public by the effective rehabilitation of high risk offenders, by tackling the causes of offending and enabling offenders to turn their lives around' (NPS, 2017). In meeting this objective, probation officers perform a wide range of

2000 Criminal Justice and Court Services Act ⬅

functions (see Box 7.1), central to which is the assessment of risk that an offender presents.

Box 7.1: Probation officer: key functions

- Providing pre-sentence reports for magistrates' courts and the Crown Court on people charged with an offence;
- Collaborating with other agencies to ensure that Multi-Agency Public Protection Arrangements (MAPPA) are effective;
- Conducting risk assessments and administering and scoring psychometric tests on offenders;
- Managing and enforcing community orders made by the courts; if offenders do not cooperate (ie breach the conditions of their order/licence), the probation officer will arrange their return to court for a further punishment.
- Motivating and changing offenders' attitudes and behaviour in order to help reduce further offending;
- Providing specialist reports to prison governors and parole review boards that help determine whether a prisoner should be released and, if so, under what conditions;
- Working with prisoners sentenced to custody during and after their sentence, to help them reintegrate into the community;
- Liaising with victims of serious crime, to keep them informed about a prisoner's progress in prison; gathering feedback about the impact of the offence; and any concerns about the proposed release of the prisoner;
- Working with other agencies to help local crime reduction and community safety, e.g. police, local authorities, courts, health services, substance misuse services, voluntary agencies and youth offending teams;
- Managing approved premises (formerly called hostels), which provide accommodation for people on bail or probation or offenders on parole.

2003 Multi-Agency Public Protection Arrangements (MAPPA) introduced ⮕

The way in which this risk is now assessed is through actuarial prediction tools and techniques such as OASys, which is the standardised assessment tool most frequently utilised by all offender managers both in prison and in the community. OASys generates a numerical score of the probability that someone will reoffend. Table 7.2 outlines the areas covered by an OASys assessment.

While the assessment of risk is firmly embedded in probation work, it is important to remember that these kinds of actuarial tools are not without their critics, who argue that these measures individualise and pathologise criminal behaviour, thereby ignoring the social and economic context of individuals' lives. The assessment criteria can be used to develop packages of intervention for offenders that are designed to address the causes of offending and to prevent recidivism, but many would argue that unless the underlying causes of crime are addressed, these kinds of interventions are at best temporary sticking plaster and at worst ineffective.

The ways in which assessment tools influence offender management is best exemplified by the types of intervention that an offender might be required to undergo as part of a community sentence, and which are managed by probation officers (see Box 7.2 for details of the orders).

Table 7.2: The OASys assessment

Scored OASys question	Specific details covered by each question
Accommodation	Of no fixed abode; suitability, permanence and location of accommodation
Employment, training and employability	Unemployment; employment history; work-related skills; attitude to employment; school attendance; problems with literacy or numeracy; any learning difficulties; any educational or professional qualifications; attitude to education or training
Relationships	Current relationship with close family; experience of childhood; current relationship with partner; previous experience of close relationships; domestic violence (perpetrator or victim); current relationship status; parental responsibilities (any problems)
Lifestyle and associates	Regular activities encourage offending; easily influenced by criminal associates; manipulative/predatory lifestyle; recklessness and risk-taking behaviour
Drug misuse	Drugs ever misused; current drug noted; level of use of main drug; ever injected drugs; motivation to tackle drug misuse; drug use and obtaining drug a major activity/occupation
Alcohol misuse	Is current use a problem; binge drinking or excessive use of alcohol in the last six months; frequency and level of alcohol misuse in the past; violent behaviour related to alcohol use at any time; motivation to tackle alcohol misuse
Thinking and behaviour	Level of interpersonal skills; impulsivity; aggressive/controlling behaviour; temper control; ability to recognise problems; problem-solving skills; awareness of consequences; achieves goals; understands other people's views; concrete/abstract thinking
Attitudes	Pro-criminal attitudes; attitude towards staff; attitude towards supervision/licence; attitude to community/society; does the offender understand their motivation for offending; motivation

Source: MacLeod et al (2012)

Box 7.2: Community orders and suspended sentence orders

In the past, offenders could be sentenced to a variety of community sentences, but there are now only two orders – the community order and the suspended sentence order:

- The community order replaced all existing community sentences for adults in 2005, and it can be imposed for a period of up to 36 months. If the conditions of the order are breached, the probation officer has the power to return the offender to court. The court can then decide to amend the order by making it more onerous, or it can revoke the sentence and resentence the offender, which may mean custody, even where the original offence was not punishable by imprisonment.
- The suspended sentence order is a custodial sentence, but if it is not breached, the sentence will be served wholly in the community. The suspended sentence order is used where the court is minded to pass a custodial sentence of less than 12 months. If the offender fails to comply with the terms of the order (breach), the court must activate the suspended sentence, unless there are strong reasons for not doing so, and the offender will be sent to prison.

The court can attach requirements to community orders or suspended sentence orders, with various possible options available (see Box 7.3). The list of requirements is almost wholly based on individualised interventions that are aimed at addressing risk factors for offending, such as drug and alcohol misuse or forms of detention such as curfews. This leads to criticisms that requirements can fail to support offenders in efforts at rehabilitation, where securing employment, dealing with debt or finding accommodation may be just as important as dealing with individual attitudes.

Typically, an order will include three or four requirements and it is the probation officer's responsibility to ensure that these are organised appropriately. This 'offender management' role does not come without challenges, however, particularly where there are many different providers involved. For example, if an offender has been given a community order with a curfew, a drug rehabilitation requirement and a Thinking Skills programme to address their attitude to offending, then four different agencies will be involved. These will: manage the tagging process (probably a private security company); provide drug rehabilitation (probably an NHS facility); run group therapy sessions (this could be a voluntary organisation); and organise the provision (the probation officer themselves). This diversity of service provision is criticised by those who argue that the capacity for rehabilitation of offenders is undermined by the fragmentation and lack of holistic approaches.

It is also the case that not all types of programmes will be accessible in all places. This has led to criticisms that some programmes might be offered to offenders because they are available and not because the programme necessarily addresses individual needs. Furthermore, in a period where all public services have seen budgets reduced, NHS services to support mental health or drug and alcohol programmes might be limited or simply unavailable. Thus, the capacity for probation officers to deliver the kinds of rehabilitation that they might wish to – or that is needed – can be constrained by factors beyond their control.

Box 7.3: Range of community order requirements

- *Unpaid work for up to 300 hours: For example, painting and decorating, gardening, environmental clean-up projects, work with charities or graffiti removal*
- *Rehabilitation activity requirement (RAR) undertaking activities as instructed*
- *Undertaking a particular programme to help change offending behavior: For example, programmes for drink-drivers, sex offenders or those who misuse drugs. Prohibition from doing particular activities: For example, attending a football match or going to a pub, on a particular day or days for a period determined by the court*
- *Adherence to a curfew, so the offender is required to be in a particular place (usually their own home) at certain times. Electronic monitoring, known as "tagging" is commonly used to enforce the curfew. An exclusion requirement, so that the offender is not allowed to go to particular places*
- *A residence requirement so that the offender is obliged to live at a particular address. This may be Approved Premises managed by the National Probation Service.*
- *A foreign travel prohibition requirement*
- *Mental health treatment with the offender's consent*
- *A drug rehabilitation requirement with the offender's consent*
- *An alcohol treatment requirement with the offender's consent*
- *An alcohol abstinence and monitoring requirement with the offender's consent*
- *Where offenders are under 25, they may be required to go to a centre at specific times over the course of their sentence.*

Source: Sentencing Council, 2017

It has been argued by Gelsthorpe and Morgan (2007) that probation's purpose in working with offenders has shifted over time – from rehabilitation to public protection, with a greater emphasis on the control elements of their job. This has meant that probation officers are now as likely to be involved in the surveillance of offenders (such as via electronic tagging) and in the enforcement of breach as they are in rehabilitative work.

This can result in the public protection aspects of the role taking priority over reducing reoffending; and means that controlling offenders and being at the front end of punishment in terms of managing community sentencing for punishment rather than rehabilitation is changing the ethos of the service.

In examining aspects of probation practice as outlined in this section, it is possible to see:

- shifts in terms of an emphasis on public protection via the assessment and management of risk rather than the welfare of the individual offender;
- a transition from unstructured, individualised clinical assessment decisions to the use of systematic and validated assessment tools;
- the increasingly systematic use of accredited packages of standardised programmes.

Key debates

The legitimacy of community punishment and offender management relies on the provision of robust probation services that can perform a dual role of ensuring public protection and the rehabilitation of offenders through community provision. This section explores the role of probation in the management of high-risk offenders in the community, which raises questions about the balance of public protection versus offenders' rights in current arrangements, before going on to examine the issues that have been raised regarding the future of community punishment arrangements under the new CRCs.

The management of high-risk offenders

The 'What works?' agenda in the 1980s suggested that probation should focus on those offenders who pose the highest level of risk of reoffending – the higher the risk, the more intensive the interventions and level of supervision that the offender requires. The new organisational structure described in this chapter clearly separates this aspect of probation work, making this the sole responsibility of the now much reduced NPS. At least three issues present themselves in the identification of high-risk offenders, including:

- designing and implementing a risk assessment tool that can reliably and consistently identify high-risk offenders;
- differing interpretations of high risk among practitioners;
- establishing sufficiently robust evidence on which to base judgements about future risk.

Predictions of 'high risk' are further complicated by the rarity of some offences and the circumstances in which they occur. For example, some circumstances in which a person commits a murder may represent a one-off event that is unlikely to happen again, and thus their risk of reoffending may be very low. In contrast, murders stemming from history of domestic violence may represent a pattern of behaviour that could well be repeated in future.

The Criminal Justice Act 2003 established statutory arrangements to manage high-risk offenders through Multi-Agency Public Protection Arrangements (MAPPA). Through MAPPA, the police, probation and prison services work together, sharing information and contributing to case management meetings – sometimes with other relevant agencies – to manage the risks posed by violent and sexual offenders living in the community. All MAPPA offenders are assessed, to establish the level of risk of harm they pose to the public, and then a plan is devised to manage those risks. Depending on the level of management, various levels of multi-agency cooperation will be required. At Level 1, most work will be done by the police and/or probation, who will share information with other agencies where necessary. At Level 2, more active multi-agency management is required, including regular MAPPA meetings. At Level 3, these meetings will involve senior members of each agency, who can authorise the use of extra resources. Table 7.3 shows that only 2% of MAPPA-eligible offenders were managed at Level 2 or Level 3 in 2016.

Table 7.3: Selected MAPPA caseload statistics, 2010-11 and 2015-16

	2010-11	2015-16
MAPPA-eligible offenders (at 31st March)	51,489	71,905
Level 1 Management	94%	98%
Proportion of Level 2 and Level 3 offenders returned to custody for breach of licence conditions	12%	15%
Number charged with a Serious Further Offence	134	193

Source: MAPPA annual reports, 2010-11 (Ministry of Justice, 2011) and 2015-16 (Ministry of Justice, 2016a)

The effective management of high-risk or 'dangerous' offenders in the community has created considerable controversy, when offenders released on licence go on to commit a further serious offence while under the supervision of probation services and/or MAPPA. Table 7.3 shows that the proportion of MAPPA offenders charged with a serious further offence is under 1% of the caseload – although substantially more are returned to custody for breach of licence conditions (around 15%).

The case of Anthony Rice highlights the potential conflict that can arise in offender management between the priority of public safety and that of due process and offender rights, and when it is appropriate to override the latter to protect victims (see Box 7.4).

Box 7.4: Serious further offence review: Anthony Rice

In October 2005, Anthony Rice was convicted of the murder of Naomi Bryant. At the time of Naomi's murder, Rice was being supervised on a Life Licence by Hampshire Probation Area and supervised under MAPPA.

The serious further offence review reported:

> we find evidence to conclude that on balance Anthony Rice should not have been released on Life Licence in the first place, and once he had been released he could and should have been better managed. This Principal Finding arises from our analysis of a complex picture where a sequence of deficiencies in the form of mistakes, misjudgements and miscommunications at all three phases of the whole process of this case had a compounding effect so that they came to amount to what we call a cumulative failure. (paragraphs 1.1.2-1.1.3)

In particular, the review found that it had been a major mistake to fail to bring forward the file from Anthony Rice's previous prison sentence, which would have shown that he was a former offender against girls as well as against adult women. It also considered that the Parole Board gave insufficient weight to the underlying nature of his risk of harm to others, because: it did not have full knowledge of his past offending behaviour, in particular that he had been an offender against children; it received cautiously encouraging, but ultimately overoptimistic, reports of Anthony Rice's progress under treatment; and its own earlier decision in 2001 to transfer him to open prison conditions set in motion a momentum towards release. The review also noted that those managing Rice's case allowed its public protection considerations to be undermined by its human rights considerations.

Source: Her Majesty's Inspectorate of Probation (2006)

Despite these concerns, research conducted for the MOJ (Peck, 2011) found that the reconviction rates of sexual and violent offenders reduced by an average of 6.5% following the introduction of MAPPA in 2001. In particular, the reconviction rates of the most high-risk offenders fell quickly after the introduction of MAPPA, supporting the idea that focusing resources on these offenders can work.

The privatisation of the management of low-risk and medium-risk offenders

As outlined earlier, there was a highly significant change in the organisation of probation services in 2014. CRCs are now responsible for the supervision of low- and medium-risk individuals on community sentences and on release from prison, leaving the NPS to manage only those high-risk offenders released from prison on licence. The rationale for these changes centres on the key philosophy of Payment by Results. What this means in practice is that the CRCs receive an upfront payment, but a large portion of their total payments will be based on the services they offer and whether they can prove that through their activities they have reduced reoffending. The potential therefore exists for the private sector to profit from punishment and in fact, therefore, indirectly to profit from crime. Such criticisms raise the question about whether such activity is ever appropriately carried out by any organisation other than a state agent.

It is too early to assess whether these new arrangements will work in terms of reducing reoffending, although early indications from Criminal Justice Joint Inspectorate reports (CJJI, 2016, 2017) suggest considerable issues with the delivery of good quality supervision (to be discussed later). The MOJ has been less than forthcoming about the costs of the programme and the anticipated savings. There are no published projections of the likely reductions in reoffending or estimates of how this might impact on the future costs of the system, so it will be difficult to assess in the future how successful the changes have been. The domination of large private sector businesses[4] in the running of CRCs – albeit in partnership with charities, third sector or public sector organisations – was to be expected, given the initial financial commitment that CRCs were expected to shoulder and the substantial size of the contracts. However, this approach might well have been at the expense of smaller local charities with a successful history of work with ex-offenders, most of whom did not have the resource to independently bid successfully for this work. In addition, in any competitive contracting exercise there is always a concern that successful bidders will simply be those that offer the cheapest price, which calls into question the quality of the service delivered.

Both CRCs and the NPS will also have to form working relationships with other local organisations, which suggests that there could be some duplication of effort, inefficient use of resources and perhaps complex accountability at a local level. Concerns have also been expressed that there could also be considerable diversity of provision and that the training and qualifications of staff working in the new CRCs may not be as robust as under the Probation Trusts earlier and will be far harder to monitor now that they are in private hands.

Over time, CRCs may come to be seen as the junior partners in probation services – particularly as they are dependent upon the NPS for the allocation of their caseload. More widely, there is a concern over the professional status and skills of those working within CRCs who will no longer carry out report writing for courts or work with high-risk offenders. These officers may well see their allocation to a CRC as a demotion and may feel that they have little opportunity for career progression. Conversely, those staff allocated to the NPS will have to deal solely with high-risk offenders and may well suffer from burnout, given the complex nature of their caseloads. There is an additional risk that CRCs may exaggerate the risk profile of some of their offenders in order to offload them onto the NPS and thus enhance the chances of success with their caseload. As recent Her Majesty's Inspectorate of Probation (HMI Probation) reports have pointed out, it will be essential that the sharing of information between the two agencies is reliable and consistent – particularly information about risk escalation, where an offender might have to move from CRC to NPS supervision. Finally, offenders are allocated to either a CRC or the NPS based on their MAPPA status and/or the risk of harm they pose. Their level of risk is assessed by a probation officer in the NPS through the Case Allocation System, and thus the CRCs will be beholden to the NPS about which offenders they are supervising.

Focus on ... the challenges of resettlement

A key aim of effective community supervision is to resettle offenders in order that they do not reoffend and are able to lead law-abiding and fulfilling lives. However, the background of most offenders means that they often have little or no experience of settled or stable lives – in terms of housing, employment or relationships. This can make it highly challenging for an offender to establish themselves in the community on release from prison.

The Labour government's 2004 Reducing Re-offending National Action Plan (Home Office, 2004) identified seven key service pathways to support released prisoners which are closely connected to the risk factors identified in the OASys assessment (see Table 7.3), and these continue to underpin resettlement screening:

- accommodation
- education, training and employment
- mental and physical health
- drugs and alcohol
- finance, benefit and debts
- children and families of offenders
- attitudes, thinking and behaviour.

Following the Corston Report (Home Office, 2007) (see Chapter Six), two further pathways specific to women offenders were added to the original seven:

- supporting women who have been abused, raped or who have experienced domestic violence
- supporting women who have been involved in prostitution.

The pathways reflect the need that prisoners may have for help with tackling the various practical problems faced on release, such as accommodation and employment, and there is also a focus on attitudes and thinking, designed to encourage self-belief in prisoners' own capacity for change.

It is important to acknowledge that the kinds of changes envisaged take time – prisoners experience many of these problems simultaneously, and so it is perhaps unrealistic to assume that a single resettlement package will provide a magic bullet. Indeed, much of the success of resettlement depends upon a continuity of case management throughout the offender's prison sentence, through the prison gate and into the community.

The establishment of NOMS (now HMPPS) aimed to reduce any discontinuity in this process, by ensuring that each offender had a whole sentence plan. The introduction of the 'Through the gate' programme in 2015[5] sought to reinvigorate the process of resettlement for all offenders, supported by provisions in the Offender Rehabilitation Act 2014, which introduced three key elements:

- First, supervision and resettlement services were extended to all prisoners who had served more than one day in custody. This provision was an attempt to address high reoffending rates among those serving short prison sentences. Its immediate effect was to increase the number of people under supervision by 50,000 cases (an increase of 25% in probation workload).
- Second, all resettlement services are provided by the new CRCs regardless of risk category – in other words, high-risk category offenders will have their resettlement package managed by the CRC while they are in prison, before transferring their post-release supervision to a probation officer in the NPS. The involvement of CRCs in resettlement was intended to generate innovative thinking around resettlement through the bidding process.
- Third, the prison estate has been reorganised to designate 89 of the 120 male prisons and all female prisons as 'resettlement prisons', where prisoners will be placed for three months before their release so that their resettlement needs can be met. Initial screening of resettlement needs is undertaken by prison officers, while the CRC is responsible for providing resettlement packages.

In principle, these provisions offer the potential for a seamless service from custody into the community, with further supervision on release offering opportunities for probation staff to continue to support individuals. However, early indications are that the system is ill-equipped to deal with the demands placed upon it. Inspections by the Criminal Justice Joint Inspectorate (CJJI) of 'Through the gate' provision in 2016 and 2017 identified a number of significant shortcomings as follows.

Resettlement provision for offenders serving 12 months or less

For offenders serving 12 months or less, the key issue was that the identification of resettlement needs by prison officers was often poor or incomplete. The inspection identified the fact that these officers were themselves often overstretched. Furthermore, the delivery of resettlement plans by CRCs was limited – action on some issues was limited to a referral to an external agency with little or no follow-up (for example, an email to a local authority housing officer for prisoners who were homeless).

The availability of services in the local community also hampers efforts at delivering resettlement – for example, the lack of affordable private rented accommodation. Specialist support with benefit claims and employment services was also limited, which exacerbates problems on release if prisoners have no income.

Resettlement provision for offenders serving over 12 months

For offenders sentenced to over 12 months, the situation was similarly problematic, despite the fact that the CRC had longer to work with offenders on their resettlement plans. There was poor identification of resettlement needs by prison staff; resettlement plans were of variable quality; and there was little or no follow-up work to ensure that released offenders engaged effectively with other services who might help.

The CJJI found that one in seven of the 98 offenders tracked were released not knowing where they would sleep that night; none were helped to enter education, training or employment after release; and only one prisoner had received support through a mentor, despite this being a key aspect of 'Through the gate' policy at the time of its introduction.

The significant issues that prisoners faced in terms of mental health or substance misuse issues were not helped by poor communication between prison and the community services that might have been able to help them on release (CJJI, 2016, 2017).

A bleak picture

Overall, the message from the most recent reviews of resettlement policy and practice are somewhat bleak, particularly against the backdrop of increasing caseloads and shrinking resources. A key issue here is the role of the CRCs in delivery of resettlement plans. The Criminal Justice Joint Inspectorate (2017) suggested that there are not sufficient incentives in the current model for CRCs to focus on resettlement, because of the way they are funded. Initial (immediate) payment for resettlement services is triggered on a 'fee-for-service' basis – once the package is delivered, the service is paid for. The quality of the resettlement package does not feature in remuneration until reoffending rates are known, at which point CRCs receive additional 'payment by results'. The problem, as identified by CJJI, is that fee-for-service payments are immediate, and so the focus has been on delivery regardless of quality – the payment for which may not arrive for at least two more years.

Furthermore, the complexity of designing resettlement plans that can account for the complex needs of many prisoners on release should not be underestimated. Desistance from crime is often described as a 'journey' that requires motivation and long-term goals and support. It often occurs 'naturally' – through the process of growing up and getting married, becoming a parent and getting a job, for example – but factors such as childhood experiences, substance misuse and previous convictions can interrupt trajectories or make it more difficult for someone to desist from crime. Current policy initiatives seek to engage with those 'non-static' factors that hold capacity for change – such as dealing with drug misuse, finding accommodation and a job – but rely heavily on the engagement of broader welfare services that reach far beyond the prison gate and for whom the pressures of austerity and rising caseloads might limit their ability to respond to ex-prisoners' needs.

Summary

- The original aims of probation lie with the Victorian temperance movement. Since its formal establishment as a criminal justice agency in 1912, the role and function of the probation service has been constantly under debate and reform.
- Significant reforms in 2014 saw the creation of 21 community rehabilitation companies that are privately contracted to provide local probation services alongside a much-reduced National Probation Service operating across six regional divisions.
- CRCs provide all services for low-/medium-risk offenders, while NPS staff are responsible for all high-risk cases. Probation officers use standardised risk assessment tools to calculate 'risk'. They have responsibility for ensuring compliance with community orders and have the power to return offenders to court or prison if they breach the conditions of their order or licence.
- Effective management of offenders in the community post-release is complex. It relies on appropriate decision making through parole boards as well as in the community, which can often rely on good quality multi-agency working.
- Much of the future success of community-based punishment will rest on the new CRCs, although it is too early to tell what the impact of the new arrangements is likely to be.

Guide to data sources and other online resources

Data used in this chapter is derived from the following sources

- NOMS annual reports and accounts for expenditure:
  https://www.gov.uk/government/publications/
  noms-annual-report-and-accounts-2015-2016
- NOMS workforce data for details of staffing:
  https://www.gov.uk/government/collections/
  national-offender-management-service-workforce-statistics
- MAPPA annual reports give details of MAPPA caseloads:
  https://www.gov.uk/government/collections/multi-agency-
  public-protection-arrangements-mappa-annual-reports
- *Offender Management Statistics Quarterly* from the MOJ shows
  details of all probation new-starts and types of supervision:
  https://www.gov.uk/government/collections/
  offender-management-statistics-quarterly

Other websites of interest

- Her Majesty's Inspectorate of Probation
  https://www.justiceinspectorates.gov.uk/hmiprobation/
- Criminal Justice Joint Inspection:
  https://www.justiceinspectorates.gov.uk/cjji/
- NOMS (to April 2017):
  https://www.gov.uk/government/organisations/
  national-offender-management-service/about
- HM Prison and Probation Service (from April 2017):
  https://www.gov.uk/government/organisations/
  her-majestys-prison-and-probation-service
- Sentencing Council:
  https://www.sentencingcouncil.org.uk/

Taking it further ...

More in-depth reading about the issues raised in this chapter

Deering, J. and Feilzer, M. (2015) *Privatising probation: Is transforming rehabilitation the end of the probation ideal?*, Bristol: Policy Press

Kemshall, H. and Maguire, M. (2001) Public protection, partnership and risk penalty: The multi-agency risk management of sexual and violent offenders, *Punishment and Society*, 3(2), 237-64

Maguire, M. and Raynor, P. (2006) How the resettlement of prisoners promotes desistance from crime: Or does it?, *Criminology & Criminal Justice*, 6(1), 19-38

Questions to consider from this chapter and your further reading

- Should all probation services be returned to state control?
- Does the MAPPA system work in protecting the public from the risk of serious offending?
- What should resettlement work prioritise to help ex-prisoners most effectively?

Notes

[1] During the Victorian period, the temperance movement advocated the prohibition of all alcohol and was connected with both religious and progressive movements. Of particular concern was the increase in drinking and drunkeness amongst the burgeoning urban working classes.

[2] Previously known as the National Offender Management Service (NOMS).

3   At the time of writing (April 2017), only NOMS annual accounts were available. In future, students will need to look at the relevant HMPPS reports to update these figures.

4   Interestingly, SERCO and G4S were banned from the bidding process following various scandals surrounding their previous MOJ contracts.

5   Towards the end of 2015, CRCs were given the responsibility to deliver a seamless resettlement service within resettlement prisons and on release. This is called the 'Through the Gate' programme.

EIGHT

Themes revisited

The preceding chapters have presented the criminal justice system as a series of independent parts – each agency has its own history, policy context, managing government department, procedures and rules. Some are even legitimate areas of substantive social science in their own right – police studies and penal studies, for example. As such, discussion of the criminal justice system as a whole can be complicated by the specific issues that are perhaps only relevant to individual agencies. In an attempt to provide a means of analysing the criminal justice *system*, this chapter seeks to address the following key questions:

- To what extent is this a 'seamless' service that provides end-to-end management of offenders?
- To what extent does the criminal justice system produce justice for all?
- What are the key drivers for policy and practice that indicate future challenges?

In doing so, the discussion revisits key themes introduced in Chapter One, drawing on the evidence presented in earlier chapters, to present a critical analysis of key aspects of criminal justice policy and practice.

Criminal justice and (in)equality

The principle of equality before the law is deeply embedded in social and cultural norms – the ways we think about 'justice' are most often associated with the idea of 'equality', but what does this mean in practice? Does it mean that everyone should be the same regardless of circumstance? This might be referred to as 'procedural justice', where the rules are applied consistently to safeguard the rights of citizens. Or does it mean that the outcomes of the process should lead to equal treatment? This is closer to what we might call 'substantive justice'.

According to Bingham's Principles of the Rule of Law (see Chapter One, Box 1.1): 'The laws of the land should apply equally to all, save to the extent that objective differences justify differentiation'. This implies that there is scope for differential treatment in particular circumstances. These issues are important to bear in mind when we are exploring inequality in criminal justice, but they can be complicated, using the term 'inequality' pejoratively – the assumption that it is always a 'bad thing', when in reality the search for substantive justice will almost always lead to differential treatment at some point in the process.

In an attempt to unravel some of the complexity surrounding 'inequality' in the criminal justice system, this concluding discussion draws on the concepts of discretion, discrimination and disproportionality (introduced in Chapter One) to explore the ways in which the practice of criminal justice can mean that people are not all treated in the same way.

Discretion

We start with an overview of the exercise of *discretion*, which features in all of the agencies described in the preceding chapters, the main features of which are summarised in Box 8.1.

Box 8.1: Examples of discretionary practice in criminal justice agencies

- **Police service** – street-level discretion by individual police officers happens at the point of arrest (whether the law has been broken)
- **Crown Prosecution Service** – the decision whether to charge and prosecute, and with what offence
- **Judiciary** – the interpretation of the law and summing up for the jury carries discretionary power, as do decisions about sentencing
- **Prison service** – prison officers have discretion over the application of rewards and incentives to prisoners and parole decisions
- **Probation** – decisions to recall offenders to prison (breach)

In exercising discretion, these decisions can lead to positive outcomes, especially if circumstances surrounding an offence would support leniency or 'mercy' – for example, in Chapter Four we saw how the Crown Prosecution Service (CPS) could use discretion in the application of the public interest test in cases of assisted suicide.

However, the basis on which discretion is applied is not always clear and this is where criticism of the criminal justice system is most often made. Therefore, it is important to consider the context within which discretion occurs – 'why' discretion occurs. To organise our analysis of this, we can draw on existing academic literature that is neatly summarised by Gelsthorpe and Padfield (2003), who suggest that there are four main variables that influence the exercise of discretion: process; environment; context; and illicit considerations. We can apply these ideas to the evidence presented in this book to examine reasons why discretion might occur across criminal justice agencies.

The process itself provides the opportunity for discretion, by giving the option for professionals to 'do nothing' rather than enforce existing rules: police officers do not have to arrest someone, the CPS can decide not to prosecute, prison officers can decide not to report prisoner behaviour, and so on. However, the criminal justice system does not operate in a social or political vacuum, and so the wider environment can influence discretionary practice through public opinion and political pressure: concerns about violence against women might encourage the CPS to be more proactive in prosecuting domestic abuse cases and for the courts to hand down harsher sentences, for example. More problematic, perhaps, is the organisational context within which discretion occurs – what are the shared values of the organisation that might influence workforce behaviour? In the case of the police, for example, the influence of cop culture might undermine attempts to address domestic abuse, if police officers believe that is not real crime. Of particular importance here is the extent to which an agency can control staff activities through robust management and disciplinary procedures – something that is difficult for senior police officers when frontline staff are operating at a distance from their oversight. Finally, there are illicit considerations – those that lead to discretion being applied based on individual characteristics such as race, gender, social class, and so on. In other words, decisions might be made on prejudicial grounds, and it is here that discretion turns into *discrimination*.

Discrimination and disproportionality

In Chapter One, we described the way in which evidence of *disproportionality* can be used to explore aspects of discretion and discrimination – that is, the way in which social groups are overrepresented or underrepresented in the criminal justice system. In this text, most of the evidence about disproportionality relates to race and ethnicity.

In Chapter Two, we saw how black individuals were overrepresented throughout the criminal justice system from arrest through to custody. Explanations for this kind of data are numerous and complex. For example, in Chapter Three we saw that the way statistics are presented in relation to stop and search by the police can make a difference to our understanding of disproportionality: when stop and search figures are based on comparisons with the resident population, BAME individuals are shown to be overrepresented; but when 'available' population rates are used, there does not appear to be any difference between black and white individuals.

So far in this discussion, we have identified the ways in which the criminal justice system allows for the exercise of discretion in various ways. In identifying the possibility of illicit considerations coming into play, we can explore evidence of overrepresentation among social groups, to consider whether this amounts to discrimination on the part of criminal justice agencies. In reality, this is difficult to prove, because there are many ways in which discretion might be exercised – not just in relation to prejudicial assumptions.

Furthermore the preceding chapters have shown that none of the agencies or professionals involved in the criminal justice system can exercise complete discretion – a whole raft of guidelines and procedures are in place to 'manage' the exercise of discretion and to remove bias (or prejudicial decision making). Examples discussed in this book include: the regulation of police powers through PACE (Chapter Three); CPS guidelines over the application of evidential and public interest tests; and sentencing guidelines for judges. All of these examples highlight the centrality of 'procedural justice' and due process throughout criminal justice policy and practice.

However, this discussion began by suggesting that procedural justice might not be enough to ensure equal treatment, and that differential treatment might be necessary in order to produce equal outcomes for individuals in different circumstances. Examples of this kind of 'substantive justice' can be seen most clearly through the treatment of women in the criminal justice system, where the application of procedural justice can lead to unfair or even harsh outcomes. In Chapter Five, the position of women in prison was explored as an example of this in practice. The relatively small number of women in prison means that the prison estate is more geographically dispersed, so women are held further away from their families than might be the case for male offenders. Combined with the high proportion of mothers who are in prison, this creates unequal outcomes for women who are unable to see their children. Even the types of offences that women are convicted of generates unequal outcomes, because they are more likely to be prosecuted by 'other agencies', such as TV Licensing, which do not have the same discretionary powers as police officers and the CPS to caution offenders instead of prosecuting them. It is these kinds of differences that lead to arguments that substantive justice for women can only be achieved by treating them differently. The *Equal Treatment Bench Book*, which provides guidance to the judiciary, acknowledges this, stating that: 'fair treatment does not mean treating everyone in the same way' (Judicial College, 2013; with 2015 amendments).

With regard to suspects and offenders, then, our brief discussion of inequality raises some complex questions about what kind of equality we want our justice system to promote, and whether the pursuit of substantive justice can be achieved within the current system where the main mechanisms for controlling bias and discretion rely on procedural rules and guidelines. Thus, promoting justice and equality before the law is not a simple exercise; it has to rely on much more than the application of rules in a fair way – it also has to be able to understand and respond to diverse needs and circumstances of offenders. One way that the criminal justice system has sought to approach this has been the diversification of the workforce – it has to reflect the society it serves.

Table 8.1: Proportion of practitioners in organisations of the criminal justice system who are women and BAME individuals (latest data)

	Police officers	CPS	Magistrates	Judges	NOMS (now HMPPS)	MOJ
Proportion of female practitioners[1]	29%	65%	53%	28%	39%	67%
Proportion of BAME practitioners[2]	6%	19%	9%	6%	6%	19%

Sources: Data from: [1] MOJ (2015c, ch 9) based on the latest data available, not necessarily collected at the same time; [2] MOJ (2014, ch 9) based on the latest data available, not necessarily collected at the same time.

To that end, we can draw on data collected by the Ministry of Justice (MOJ) to consider workforce diversity across each of the agencies (see Table 8.1).

It is clear from the diversity data that some agencies have more diverse workforces than others – both the CPS and the MOJ employ proportionately more women and black and minority ethnic (BAME) individuals, for example. However, the low proportions of BAME individuals in all agencies suggests that attempts to make the criminal justice more representative are not succeeding – particularly in key areas such as the police and the judiciary, where the application of discretion might produce the most serious outcomes for individuals.

Consequently, there are important observations to be made about aspects of disproportionality in workforce statistics, some of which were rehearsed in Chapter Five, where diversity among the judiciary was explored in more detail:

- First, the agencies need to attract people to apply for positions. In some areas of work this can be hindered by a lack of prior qualifications (for the judiciary, for example) or community resistance (BAME–police relations might prevent people from wanting to be part of the organisation, for example).
- Second, working conditions might also affect the likelihood of increasing diversity – shift patterns in the prison and police service can deter women, for example.
- Third, a lack of opportunities for promotion or advancement might affect staff retention in agencies, especially when proportions of senior staff in most criminal justice agencies are significantly lower for women and BAME individuals than overall proportions shown here.

Understanding aspects of inequality in criminal justice is therefore complex and multifaceted. If we are interested in justice for offenders, we need to be alert to how discretion operates among criminal justice practitioners and whether this generates discrimination for some social groups. At the same time, we need to consider how substantive justice can be realised for those whose circumstances require alternative approaches to criminal justice, so that we can ensure that outcomes are not worse for some social groups. Assuming that increasing diversity within professions can support occupational or cultural change across the system may be naive, however, given the persistent dominance of white males throughout criminal justice.

A criminal justice system?

Throughout this book, we have made reference to the 'criminal justice system' – a widely used term but one that implies working arrangements that are not necessarily aligned with reality. If we think about the fictitious case study example of Jimmy in Chapter Two, he passed through a series of agencies, each of which was responsible for part of an overall criminal justice process from arrest to prosecution and then on to trial, conviction, custody and finally release. At each stage of the process, different people working in different organisations with different aims and objectives will have been responsible for Jimmy's case. Each of these agencies operates different systems for recording offenders, and huge amounts of paper will have been used to generate files for his appearance in court, let alone the organisation required to make sure that Jimmy was transported from the police station to the magistrates' court and then to prison and then to trial … and so on. In the course of this one case, Jimmy might have come into contact with private contractors and voluntary organisations alongside numerous public officials and practitioners. At each point that Jimmy transferred from one of these organisations to another, there is the potential for something to go wrong. A piece of paper is missing, his name is not on the list where it should be, someone forgot to send a file, the transport to court was running late … the possibilities for small errors are endless. Yet these small failures across many, many cases lead to major difficulties for the criminal justice process in terms of cost, efficiency and effectiveness.

There are good reasons why successive governments have been concerned about the 'system' of criminal justice hinted at here. First, there are concerns to create a system that can reduce delays in the administration of justice to generate efficiency; this not only benefits the public purse by reducing costs, but also alleviates pressure on victims, witnesses and suspects, for whom long delays can be harmful. Second, creating a system where aims and objectives are shared from start to end and where offenders are managed appropriately should improve outcomes – in particular by reducing reoffending.

Current policy and practice aim to promote both of these results – an efficient, seamless service that is effective in reducing reoffending through appropriate management of offenders. The mechanisms currently promoted to achieve this fall into three main areas:

- better joined-up working between agencies to reduce duplication and to improve information sharing;
- reduce bureaucracy (paperwork) and complexity to speed up processes and improve experiences for victims and witnesses;
- provide 'end-to-end' management of offenders to reduce reoffending.

We can examine each of these and consider what the evidence we have presented in the preceding chapters tells us about the barriers that might exist for these aims to be realised.

Promoting joined-up working

The lack of 'joined up working' and collaboration between agencies in criminal justice has been of concern for a number of years. Since the 1980s, there has been a belief in the need for better collaboration across public organisations generally, not just in criminal justice, to generate more effective solutions to intractable social problems.

In criminal justice, the need for collaboration across agencies is especially important, when the decisions or actions taken at one point in the process impact on those agencies further down the process. So, for example, the decision of the police to arrest someone in the belief that an offence has been committed will ultimately require action on the part of the CPS to charge – their decision will affect in which court the case is heard and, ultimately, what kind of punishment an offender will receive. The parts of the process are intertwined and mutually reliant, so collaboration and joined-up working can help to generate efficient and effective outcomes. In Chapter Four, we discussed the use of Statutory Charging Schemes that were introduced to address the problems that occurred through 'overcharging' (charging someone for a more serious offence than is warranted), which necessarily requires the CPS and the police to work collaboratively.

The need for better collaboration between agencies is not just about relationships between criminal justice practitioners, but extends to all those professionals who may come into contact with offenders and victims. At a local level, for example, police and crime commissioners (see Chapter Three) have responsibility for ensuring that all agencies with an interest in crime-related issues are brought together to develop crime plans and initiatives. Many of these agencies lie far beyond criminal justice, such as health or education.

However, there are limits to collaboration. One of the central tenets of the criminal justice system is that each agency operates independently in order to ensure fairness – each agency, in effect, provides a check on the decisions that were made in earlier parts of the process. Too much collaboration and joined-up working could undermine a key element of accountability that runs through the process.

Also, the extensive network of private and voluntary organisations that are increasingly involved in a mixed economy of criminal justice raises questions about the capacity for cooperation and collaboration in a competitive environment. In probation, for example, the need for practitioners to operate across private and public sector prisons and private sector community rehabilitation companies (CRCs) alongside public sector probation officers suggests a fragmented service framework rather than a collaborative system.

Reducing bureaucracy

The second area where policy has sought to promote efficiency in the justice system is through reducing bureaucracy and simplifying complex processes. Primarily this has meant investment in technology, particularly through the prosecution process. New 'digital courtrooms' are being developed, which have the capacity for defendants on remand to appear via video link from prison and for all case paperwork to be available on digital devices rather than on paper.

To a student in a 21st-century college or university this hardly sounds like a revolution, but the age of most court buildings, combined with lack of investment and capacity in digital technology, makes these developments (for some at least) long overdue. However, developments in technology are costly – the MOJ has invested over £160 million in the digital courtroom programme, and there are still challenges that will need to be faced for the revolution to succeed, not least from among the judiciary, some of whom are concerned that the application of justice needs to be face to face.

Providing end-to-end management

The third area of concern for policy makers is to reduce reoffending. A system that operates to common objectives with clear offender management processes is believed to be the best way to do this. The most recent changes to how offenders are managed (as outlined in the government document 'Transforming Rehabilitation' (MOJ, 2013)) have expanded post-release supervision to all those leaving the prison system, for example. However, the 'Focus on ... resettlement' discussion in Chapter Seven also identified problems with practitioner engagement with elements of the new system, which require staff from across the prison service, CRCs and the probation service to share information effectively. Furthermore, successful resettlement and offender supervision in the community relies on many external agencies that provide the wider services that many offenders need:

health, housing, social care, social security, and so on. Without their support, end-to-end management and resettlement plans simply fail.

Thinking about criminal justice as a system allows us to consider the ways in which policy and practice support or undermine efforts to create efficient and effective processes that can provide a positive experience for victims and witnesses and enable rehabilitation for offenders. To operate as a system in this way requires: clear policy objectives that are shared across agencies; investment in technology to maintain efficiency; and joined-up working between practitioners and policy makers. In an arena where there are many competing interests and complex decisions made by numerous practitioners operating with varying degrees of professional discretion, it is little wonder that the search for a seamless system continues.

Policy directions

Chapter One provided a brief overview of the broad political trends that dominate contemporary analysis of criminal justice policy, focusing on some key features of a 'new consensus' from the early 1990s. Our discussion in subsequent chapters has provided examples of these features in practice, most notably in relation to dangerous offenders through mechanisms such as MAPPA and the focus on persistent offending through priorities in rehabilitation. However, a significant contextual issue that is not reflected in the 'new consensus' is the impact of austerity measures since 2010, which show little sign of abating. All of the agencies we have discussed in this book have witnessed significant reductions in expenditure that have consequences for all areas of the criminal justice process.

Some of the impacts of these funding cuts have been identified in the preceding chapters. They include the following:

- **Workforce reductions** – all agencies have seen changes in staffing levels. In some areas, such as the police and prison service, the staff cuts have been severe enough to raise concerns of workforce crisis. The impact of reducing staff levels can be serious when security and safety are compromised, as they can be in prison for example, but they are also felt throughout the system – when staff do not have time to manage caseloads or complete risk assessments, and so on. These are the kinds of issues that inspectorate reports in all criminal justice agencies often highlight, giving you the opportunity to follow these up over the next few years.

- **Estate reforms** – the physical assets of the criminal justice system are also changing in response to austerity. Courts have been closed, and old prison buildings that are expensive to run have been decommissioned and replaced with new buildings. This means that the landscape and geography of criminal justice is changing – lots of towns no longer have local courts, and bigger prisons are being built to house prisoners for the majority of their sentence before they are sent to local resettlement prisons in advance of their release.
- **Doing more for less** – some agencies, like the CPS, have seen their remit expanding – taking on responsibility for victims and witnesses, for example – while losing resources; in others, such as the court service, technology is being used to reduce operating costs as well as to improve efficiency.

Within this overall impact has been an underlying trend towards a *mixed economy of criminal justice*. This book has highlighted three examples where the mixed economy operates: private prison estate, community rehabilitation companies, and voluntary sector provision of women's centres for female offenders. Each of these exemplifies different aspects of the debates that continue to rage about the influence of non-state agencies in criminal justice.

The private prison sector is now firmly embedded in mainstream provision and is unlikely to disappear. However, concerns continue to be raised in inspectorate reports and other data about aspects of security and safety in private prisons. Lines of accountability between private companies and government departments also remain problematic, particularly in relation to the quality of control over contracts in the aftermath of fraud involving overcharging by private sector companies.

It is too early to give any indication as to the success of private probation services run through the new CRCs, but initial indications are that there are likely to be similar issues around contractual arrangements and incentive schemes such as Payment by Results. Accountability for CRCs is also more difficult than for the private prison sector, since HMI Probation has no statutory power to conduct inspections. A significant concern will be whether or not CRCs are sustainable if current offender profiles (which are tending towards the more serious) continue, thereby reducing the overall 'supply' of caseloads.

Finally, in a climate of austerity, the capacity of the voluntary sector to maintain funding for its wide range of support activities is always threatened. In Chapter Six, our discussion of women's centres showed that, despite their effectiveness, funding cuts have meant changes to how they provide services and to whom.

This book has attempted to provide you with various tools that you can use to interrogate aspects of criminal justice policy and practice as you move through your studies. Making use of conceptual frameworks such as discretion, discrimination, equality and justice provide a lens through which you can test the ways in which the criminal justice system operates. Adopting a critical perspective about policy and practice will enable you to think about how the aims and objectives of these agencies promote particular ideas about justice – and who the justice system serves. Above all, we hope to inspire you to go beyond the facts, to make use of all the data freely available to you and to keep asking questions.

References

Auld, Right Honourable Lord Justice (2001) *Review of the criminal courts of England and Wales: Report* (The Auld Commission), London: TSO

Bingham, T. (2010) *The rule of law*, London: Allen Lane

Brownlee, I.D., (2004) 'The statutory charging scheme in England and Wales: towards a unified prosecution system?', *Criminal Law Review*, 896-907

Burton, M. (2001) 'Reviewing Crown Prosecution Service decisions not to prosecute', *Criminal Law Review,* 374-84

Butler, His Honour Gerald QC (1999) *Inquiry into Crown Prosecution Service decision-making in relation to deaths in custody and related matters*, London: The Stationery Office

CJJI (Criminal Justice Joint Inspectorate) (2015) *Joint Inspection of the provision of charging decisions*, London: HMCPSI/HMIC.

CJJI (2016) *An Inspection of Through the Gate Resettlement Services for Short-Term Prisoners*, London: CJJI

CJJI (2017) *An Inspection of Through the Gate Resettlement Services for Prisoners Serving 12 Months or More*, London: CJJI

College of Policing (2014) *The Code – Policing principles*. www.college.police.uk/What-we-do/Ethics/Pages/Code-of-Ethics.aspx

CPS(Crown Prosecution Service) (2013) *The Code for Crown Prosecutors*, London: CPS. https://www.cps.gov.uk/publications/code_for_crown_prosecutors

CPS (2013) *The Director's guidance on charging 2013* (5th edn) (revised arrangements), London: CPS. https://www.cps.gov.uk/publications/directors_guidance/dpp_guidance_5.html

CPS (2015) *Annual report and accounts 2014-15*, London: CPS

CPS (2016) *Violence against women and girls: Crime Report 2015-16*, London: CPS. www.cps.gov.uk/publications/docs/cps_vawg_report_2016.pdf

Deering, J. and Feilzer, M. (2015) *Privatising probation: Is transforming rehabilitation the end of the probation ideal?*, Bristol: Policy Press

Director of Public Prosecutions (2016) Victims' Right to Review Guidance, London: Crown Prosecution Service. http://www.cps.gov.uk/publications/docs/vrr_guidance_2016.pdf

Downes, D. and Morgan, R. (2002) The skeletons in the cupboard: The politics of law and order at the turn of the millennium, in M. Maguire, R. Morgan and R. Reiner (eds) *Oxford handbook of criminology* (3rd edn), Oxford: Oxford University Press

Garside, R. (2014) *The coming probation privatisation disaster*, London: Centre for Crime and Justice Studies. https://www.crimeandjustice.org.uk/resources/coming-probation-privatisation-disaster

Gelsthorpe, L. and Morgan, R. (2007) *Handbook of probation*, London: Routledge

Gelsthorpe, L. and Padfield, N. (2003) *Exercising discretion: Decision making in the criminal justice system and beyond*, Cullompton: Willan Publishing

Gladstone Committee (1895) *Report from the Departmental Committee on Prisons*, Parliamentary papers, vol lvi

Her Majesty's Courts and Tribunals Service (2016) *Annual Report and Accounts 2015-16*, London: HMSO

HMCPSI (Her Majesty's Crown Prosecution Service Inspectorate) (2007) *Discontinuance: Thematic review of the decision-making and management in discontinued cases and discharged committals summative report based on the rolling programme of Casework Quality Assessment undertaken in eight CPS areas*, London: HMCPSI

HMCPSI (2012) *Follow up report of the thematic review of the quality of prosecution advocacy and case presentation*, London: HMCPSI

HMCPSI (2015) *Thematic review of the CPS advocacy strategy and progress against the recommendations of the follow-up report of the quality of prosecution advocacy and case presentation*, London: HMCPSI

HMIC (2015) *Integrity matters: An inspection of arrangements to ensure integrity and to provide the capability to tackle corruption in policing*. https://www.justiceinspectorates.gov.uk/hmicfrs/wp-content/uploads/police-integrity-and-corruption-2015.pdf

HMIP (2006) *An independent review of a serious further offence case: Anthony Rice*. https://www.justiceinspectorates.gov.uk/probation/wp-content/uploads/sites/5/2014/03/anthonyricereport-rps.pdf

Home Office (2004) *Reducing Re-offending National Action Plan*, London: Home Office Communication Directorate

Home Office (2007) *The Corston report: A report by Baroness Jean Corston of a review of women with particular vulnerabilities in the criminal justice system*, London: Home Office

House of Commons Home Affairs Committee (2016) *Police diversity*, London: House of Commons

House of Commons Justice Committee (2009) *The Crown Prosecution Service: Gatekeeper of the criminal justice system*, London: HCJC

Johnston, N. and Politowski, B. (2016) *Police funding*, House of Commons Library Briefing Paper Number 7279. researchbriefings.files.parliament.uk/documents/CBP-7279/CBP-7279.pdf

Judicial Appointments Commission (2013) *Barriers to application to judicial appointments*, London: JAC

Judicial College (2013, with 2015 amendments) *Equal treatment bench book*. https://www.judiciary.gov.uk/publications/equal-treatment-bench-book/

MacLeod, J., Grove, P. and Farrington, D. (2012) *Explaining criminal careers*, Oxford: OUP

Macpherson, W. (1999) *The Stephen Lawrence inquiry*, London: Home Office

Martinson, R. (1974) 'What works? Questions and answers about prison reform', *The Public Interest*, 35, 22-54

McConville, M., Sanders, A. and Leng, R. (1993) *The case for the prosecution: Police suspects and the construction of criminality*, London: Routledge

McLaughlin, E., Muncie, J. and Hughes, G. (2001) 'The permanent revolution: New Labour, new public management and the modernisation of criminal justice', *Criminal Justice*, 1(3), 301-18

MOJ (Ministry of Justice) (2002) *Justice for all*, London: The Stationery Office

MOJ (2011) *Multi-Agency Public Protection Arrangements: Annual Report 2010/11: Ministry of Justice Statistics bulletin*. London: MOJ. https://www.gov.uk/government/uploads/system/uploads/attachment_data/file/218060/mappa-annual-report-10-11.pdf

MOJ (2013) *Transforming Rehabilitation: A Stategy for Reform*, London: MOJ.

MOJ (2014) Statistics on race and the criminal justice system. https://www.gov.uk/government/collections/race-and-the-criminal-justice-system

MOJ (2015) *Statistics on race and the criminal justice system 2014*, London: MOJ. www.gov.uk/government/statistics/race-and-the-criminal-justice-system-2014

MOJ (2015a) *Code of Practice for Victims of Crime*. London: HMSO

MOJ (2015b) *Female offenders and child dependents*. https://www.gov.uk/go vernment/statistics/female-offenders-and-child-dependents

MOJ (2015c) *Women and the criminal justice system*. https://www.gov.uk/government/statistics/women-and-the-criminal-justice-system-statistics-2015

MOJ (2016) *Prison safety and reform*, Cmd 9350, London: MOJ

MOJ (2016a) *Multi-Agency Public Protection Arrangements annual report 2015/16: Ministry of Justice Statistics Bulletin*. London: Ministry of Justice. https://www.gov.uk/government/uploads/system/uploads/attachment_data/file/563117/MAPPA_Annual_Report_2015-16.pdf

MOJ (2017) *Proven Reoffending Statistics Quarterly Bulletin, July 2014 to June 2015*. https://www.gov.uk/government/uploads/system/uploads/attachment_data/file/611174/proven-reoffending-2015-q2.pdf

Minson, S., Nadin, R. and Earle, J. (2015) *Sentencing of mothers: Improving the sentencing process and outcomes for women with dependent children*, London: Prison Reform Trust

National Appropriate Adult Network (2015) *There to help: Ensuring provision of appropriate adults for mentally vulnerable adults detained or interviewed by the police*. www.appropriateadult.org.uk/images/pdf/2015_theretohelp_complete.pd

National Audit Office (2013) *Managing the prison estate*. https://www.nao.org.uk/report/managing-the-prison-estate

National Audit Office (2015) *A short guide to the Home Office*, London: TSO

Neuberger, Baroness (2010) *Report of the Advisory Panel on Judicial Diversity*, London: Ministry of Justice

Newburn, T. (2015*) Literature review: Police integrity and corruption*, London: HMIC

NPS (National Probation Service) (2017), https://www.gov.uk/government/organisations/national-probation-service/about#our-responsibilities

Packer, H. (1968) *The limits of the criminal sanction*, Stanford, CA: Stanford University Press

Peck, M. (2011) *Patterns of reconviction among offenders eligible for Multi-Agency Public Protection Arrangements (MAPPA)*, London: Ministry of Justice

Prison Reform Trust (2016) *Bromley Briefings Prison Factfile*, Autumn. http://www.prisonreformtrust.org.uk/Portals/0/Documents/Bromley%20Briefings/Autumn%202016%20Factfile.pdf

Prison Reform Trust (2017*) What can I do? Your guide to achieving change in the criminal justice system*. http://www.prisonreformtrust.org.uk/Portals/0/Documents/What%20Can%20I%20Do.pdf

Reiner, R. (2010) *Politics of the police* (4th edn), Oxford: Oxford University Press

Scarman, Lord Justice (1981) *The Brixton disorders, 10-12th April (1981)*, London: HMSO

Sentencing Council (2016) *Reduction in sentence for a guilty plea guideline: Consultation*, London: Sentencing Council

Sentencing Council (2017) *Imposition of Community and Custodial Sentences: Definitive Guideline*, London: Sentencing Council

Starmer, K. (Director of Public Prosecutions) (2010) 'The suicide of Mr Raymond Cutkelvin – decision on prosecution', London: CPS. www.cps.gov.uk/news/articles/the_suicide_of_mr_raymond_cutkelvin_decision_on_prosecution/

UNODC (United Nations Office on Drugs and Crime) (2015) *The United Nations Standard Minimum Rules for the Treatment of Prisoners* (the Nelson Mandela Rules). https://www.unodc.org/documents/justice-and-prison-reform/GA-RESOLUTION/E_ebook.pdf

Wilks-Wiffen, S. (2011) *Voice of a child*, London: Howard League for Penal Reform

Women in Prison (2017) *Corston +10: The Corston Report 10 years on. How far have we come on the road to reform for women affected by the criminal justice system?*, London: Women in Prison

Woolf, Lord Justice (1991) *Prison disturbances April 1990: Report of an Inquiry by the Right Honourable Lord Justice Woolf (parts 1 and 2) and His Honour Judge Stephen Tumin (part 2)*, London: HMSO

APPENDIX 1

Home Secretaries since 1945

Home Secretary	Dates of office	Political party	Prime Minister
James Ede	3 August 1945-26 October 1951	Labour	Clement Attlee
David Fyfe	27 October 1951-19 October 1954	Conservative	Winston Churchill
Gwilym Lloyd George	19 October 1954-14 January 1957	Liberal and Conservative	Anthony Eden
R A Butler	14 January 1957-13 July 1962	Conservative	Anthony Eden
Henry Brooke	14 July 1962-16 October 1964	Conservative	Sir Alec Douglas Home
Sir Frank Soskice	18 October 1964-23 December 1965	Labour	Harold Wilson
Roy Jenkins	23 December 1965-30 November 1967	Labour	Harold Wilson
James Callaghan	30 November 1967-19 June 1970	Labour	Harold Wilson
Reginald Maudling	20 June 1970-18 July 1972	Conservative	Edward Heath
Robert Carr	18 July 1972-4 March 1974	Conservative	Edward Heath
Roy Jenkins	5 March 1974-10 September 1976	Labour	Harold Wilson

Merlyn Rees	10 September 1976- 4 May 1979	Labour	James Callaghan
William Whitelaw	4 May 1979- 11 June 1983	Conservative	Margaret Thatcher
Leon Brittan	11 June 1983- 2 September 1985	Conservative	Margaret Thatcher
Douglas Hurd	2 September 1985- 26 October 1989	Conservative	Margaret Thatcher
David Waddington	26 October 1989- 28 November 1990	Conservative	Margaret Thatcher
Kenneth Baker	28 November 1990- 10 April 1992	Conservative	John Major
Kenneth Clarke	10 April 1992- 27 May 1993	Conservative	John Major
Michael Howard	27 May 1993- 2 May 1997	Conservative	John Major
Jack Straw	2 May 1997- 8 June 2001	Labour	Tony Blair
David Blunkett	8 June 2001- 15 December 2004	Labour	Tony Blair
Charles Clarke	15 December 2004- 5 May 2006	Labour	Tony Blair
John Reid	5 May 2006- 27 June 2007	Labour	Tony Blair
Jacqui Smith	28 June 2007- 5 June 2009	Labour	Gordon Brown
Alan Johnson	5 June 2009- 11 May 2010	Labour	Gordon Brown
Theresa May	12 May 2010- 13 July 2016	Conservative	David Cameron
Amber Rudd	13 July 2016- *incumbent*	Conservative	Theresa May

APPENDIX 2

Justice Secretaries since 2007

Name	Dates of office	Political party	Prime Minister
The Lord Falconer of Thoroton	9 May 2007-27 June 2007	Labour	Tony Blair
Jack Straw	28 June 2007-11 May 2010	Labour	Gordon Brown
Kenneth Clarke	12 May 2010-4 September 2012	Conservative	David Cameron
Chris Grayling	4 September 2012-9 May 2015	Conservative	David Cameron
Michael Gove	9 May 2015-14 July 2016	Conservative	David Cameron
Elizabeth Truss	14 July 2016-11 June 2017	Conservative	Theresa May
David Lidington	11 June 2017-*incumbent*	Conservative	Theresa May

APPENDIX 3

Key dates and events

The criminal justice process – key dates and events

Date	Event/Notes
1779	Penitentiary Act – promotes idea of prison for 'reform' of offenders
1829	Metropolitan Police Service established
1842	Pentonville Prison opens – the first 'modern prison' based on a panopticon design (Jeremy Bentham)
1967	Criminal Justice Act – introduces parole
1981	Royal Commission on Criminal Procedure – recommends radical reform of police powers and changing the process of prosecution culminating in the establishment of PACE and the CPS
1984	Police and Criminal Evidence Act (PACE) – reform of police powers
1985	Prosecution of Offences Act – introduces the CPS
2000	Criminal Justice and Court Services Act – reform of the probation service to a more centralised system
2004	Establishment of National Offender Management System (NOMS) – merges together prison and probation service to provide end to end management of offenders
2005	Constitutional Reform Act – establishes Supreme Court
2007	Ministry of Justice formed
2010	Breaking the Cycle Green Paper introduces concept of 'payment by results' within the criminal justice system

Date	Event/Notes
2013	Criminal Justice Board meets for the first time
2013	Transforming Rehabilitation White Paper
2014	Offender Rehabilitation Act – introduction of Community Rehabilitation Companies into the probation service

Police – key dates and events

Date	Event/Notes
1829	Metropolitan Police Improvement Act – establishes 'new' police in London
1856	County and Boroughs Police Act – provides for the establishment of regional police forces
1856	Establishment of HM Inspectorate of Constabulary
1878	Criminal Investigation Department of the Metropolitan Police established
1960	Royal Commission on the Police
1964	Police Act – establishes tri-partite structure of police governance
1974	Introduction of Police National Computer which allows police forces to share basic information about criminals for the first time
1976	Police Act – Establishes the Police Complaints Board (PCB) (operational 1977)
1981	Scarman Report on riots in Brixton published – critical of poor relations between police and ethnic minority communities. Critical of use of stop and search
1984	Police and Criminal Evidence Act – introduces codes of practice relating to police powers and investigations
1985	Police Complaints Authority replaces PCB
1993	Murder of Stephen Lawrence
1994	Police and Magistrates Courts Act – introduces new funding arrangements for police. Home Secretary given powers to set objectives for the Police Service
1999	Macpherson Report published
2001	Police Service of Northern Ireland replaces Royal Ulster Constabulary (RUC)
2002	Police Reform Act – Independent Police Complaints Commission (IPCC) established to replace PCA. Introduction of PCSOs and Designated Officers

2010	Crime and Security Act – reduces the reporting requirements for stop and search powers
2011	Police Reform and Social Responsibility Act – transfers police accountability to Police Crime Commissioners
2012	First Police Crime Commissioner Elections
2012	College of Policing established
2013	Crime and Courts Act – establishes National Crime Agency
2013	Police Scotland replaces 8 regional forces with a single unified force
2017	Policing and Crime Act – reforms to complaints system to help whistleblowers and introduction of 'super-complaints'. Extends disciplinary procedures to those who have left the force

Prosecution – key dates and events

Date	Event
1829	Metropolitan Police Act – police adopt responsibility for first public prosecutions
1880	First Director of Public Prosecutions appointed to deal with serious cases
1981	Royal Commission on Criminal Procedure – recommends separating investigation of crime (police) from prosecution of cases
1985	Prosecution of Offences Act – establishes Crown Prosecution Service (operational 1986)
1998	Glidewell Report – recommends changes to work and structure of CPS
2001	Auld Commission
2002	Justice for All White Paper
2003	Criminal Justice Act – introduces Statutory Charging Scheme
2013	Victims Right to Review introduced – allows victims the right to appeal against CPS decision not to prosecute
2015	Victims Code of Practice introduced and updated

Criminal Courts – key dates and events

Date	Event
1166	Declaration at the Assize of Clarendon – establishes Assizes system for trials to be held around the country
1967	Criminal Justice Act – introduces majority verdict jury
1971	Courts Act – establishes Crown Court. Abolishes Assizes and Quarter Sessions

1972	Criminal Justice Act – composition of juries expanded to all persons on electoral role aged 16–65
1974	Juries Act – imposes upper age limit of 70 on jury service
1980	Magistrates Court Act
1994	Police and Magistrates Court Act – changes organisation and funding of magistrates courts
1997	Criminal Cases Review Commission begins operating
1999	Youth Justice and Criminal Evidence Act – introduces use of screens, live link CCTV and use of pre-recorded interviews in court to support vulnerable witnesses
1999	Launch of the Equal Treatment Bench Book
2001	Auld Review
2001	Commission for Judicial Appointments established
2003	Courts Act – establishes local justice areas overseen by HM Courts Service. Establishes new HM Inspectorate of Court Administration
2003	Criminal Justice Act – establishes Sentencing Guidelines Council and establishes aim of sentencing in statute
2004	Appointment of the first female Law Lord (Brenda Hale)
2005	Constitutional Reform Act – establishes Supreme Court of the UK to replace the appeal role of the House of Lords
2009	Coroners and Justice Act – provides for live video links and screens around witness box to protect vulnerable and intimidated witnesses
2013	Crime and Courts Act – introduces 'efficiency and transparency' measures to courts and tribunals. Introduces reform of judicial appointments system
2014	Legal Aid, Sentencing and Punishment of Offenders Act – new sentencing powers for knife crime and causing injury by dangerous driving; more restrictive curfews and longer supervision; more life sentences for dangerous offenders

Probation Service – key dates and events

Date	Event
1907	Probation of Offenders Act
1936	HM Inspectorate of Probation established
1973	Community service introduced as alternative punishment to prison
1974	Robert Martinson publishes his study 'What works', which generates the 'Nothing works' agenda critical of prisoner rehabilitation programmes

1991	Criminal Justice Act
1992	Introduction of national standards for probation service ending discretion afforded probation officers
1999	Publication of 'What Works? Reducing reoffending: Evidence based practice' advocating accredited programmes
2000	Criminal Justice and Court Services Act – creates National Probation Service
2003	Multi-Agency Public Protection Arrangements (MAPPA) introduced
2003	Carter Report – advocates amalgamation of prison and probation service
2004	National Offender Management Service (NOMS) becomes operational
2007	Offender Management Act – introduces principle of sub-contracting of probation services from public, private or voluntary organisations. Replaced Probation Boards with 35 Probation Trusts
2014	Offender Rehabilitation Act – replaces probation trusts with single National Probation Service and 21 Community Rehabilitation Companies (privately contracted)

Index

References to tables and figures are shown in *italics*